A Pearl of Great Value

One Man's Journey of Faith
Based on Interviews with
Tom Halliburton

Foreword by Jacob Armstrong

Tricia Cundiff

A Pearl of Great Value © 2025 by Tricia Cundiff.

All rights reserved. No part of this book may be reproduced in any form or by any electronic or mechanical means, including information storage and retrieval systems, without permission in writing from the author. The only exception is by a reviewer, who may quote short excerpts in a review.

ISBN 979-8-9939003-1-5

This book is based on interviews between the author and Tom Halliburton, recorded from January 2025 through August 2025. Neither the author nor the contributors shall be held liable for any suggestions or information contained in this book.

Tricia Cundiff
Visit my website at www.TriciaCundiff.com

Printed in the United States of America

First Printing: December 2025

One of my favorite scriptures is Matthew 13:45-46, the parable of the Pearl of Great Value. It's about a merchant. When he finds a Pearl of Great Value, he sells everything he owns so that he can buy it. I take that in a different direction than most. I guess most people don't think of it this way. If you asked most people what the Pearl of Great Value is, they would answer Jesus. I understand how they feel that way.

Years ago, I felt God ask me to list all of the things of value that I had given up to serve Him. There was nothing there. Nothing I had given up had any value. Jesus considers me a Pearl of Great Value. While no one else may have thought that I had any value, He did. He gave up everything for me. He was beaten. He died for me. To Him, I was a Pearl of Great Value. There's nobody in this world who would ever consider me of any value. But Jesus did.

- Tom Halliburton
May 14, 2025

For Tom and Gayle,

Your words and your love for Jesus

Have made this journey beautiful.

AUTHOR'S NOTE

The hours I spent with Tom Halliburton were blessings (I hesitate to call them interviews; they were more like conversations between friends); I hope there will be many more. The gifts I received in those times have soothed me, inspired me, assured me, and caused me to yearn for a deeper walk with Jesus.

My fear, my struggle with this book, is that I cannot possibly capture the passion and deep emotion that Tom conveys when he talks about his walk with the Lord. How to put into words the way his voice would sometimes tremble, the rise and fall of its timbre, the veracity of truth that poured forth from this man whom God chose to be a pastor.

Tracing the journey through the valleys and mountains of Tom's life has been an ongoing blessing. I pray the following pages will do his story justice and portray the man who has inspired me and multitudes of others to follow Jesus.

Words from a Harley Davidson ad come to mind – and bear repeating: "When writing the story of your life, never let anyone else hold the pen." The story you will read is Tom's. Direct quotes from Tom are in italics throughout, and he has reviewed every word to ensure that it is, indeed, his story. Some names have been changed; an asterisk designates them.

A Pearl of Great Value is a different kind of story, a true story of a reckoning and a triumph. I am honored to call Tom and Gayle Halliburton friends. I have no doubt you will be blessed that Tom has agreed to share his life with you, with us.

FOREWORD

I knew of Tom Halliburton before I knew Tom Halliburton. I knew he was a leader. I knew he was a man filled with the Spirit. I knew he both worshipped passionately and cared for those in need. I knew that his faith in Jesus had a direct correlation to how he lived his life and how he served others. Without knowing Tom personally, as a young pastor, he was the kind of pastor I wanted to be.

When I got to know Tom, I realized that the fire that burned bright in his ministry was actually cultivated from a deep, abiding relationship with his Lord, Jesus Christ. I met what everyone meets in Tom, a man who is fun, funny, and while exhibiting a tough exterior actually is a very tender man who loves and cares for people deeply.

I feel honored that Tom took me in as a mentee. He was my boss, but he always made it clear that our relationship was about much more than our professional life. He cared for me and my family. He took us out for meals, gave my daughters gifts, and let us borrow their camper for vacations. Tom became my friend.

Tom is impressive. He can open the Bible to any page and teach an hour Bible Study on it. He can stand to preach with no notice and bring Jesus into the room. Tom is an impressive leader with natural gifting to bring unity out of division and peace where there is chaos. Tom is impressive but Tom impressed on me to always keep Jesus as the center. To keep Jesus as the center of my life and the center of the church. And Tom has lived a life in connection with and service to Jesus. He has pastored at every level and held leadership roles locally and globally. But, in all of it, Tom never has forgotten that Jesus saved his soul and He is worthy of all of our honor and praise.

As you read about Tom's life you will marvel at all the places he has gone and all the things he has done. You will marvel at his love for God and his love for people as a husband, father, and pastor. Tom can tell a story. You will love hearing his stories and his story in this book. I think most of his stories are true, though maybe the fishing stories are a bit exaggerated. As you read, picture yourself sitting at the feet of a great storyteller. And pay close attention because the story he is telling is actually the story of Jesus in his life. I know that Tom would want you as you read, to keep Jesus at the center. Look for Him in the pages of Tom's story.

- Jacob Armstrong, Lead Pastor
Providence Church

PROLOGUE

"The time came when I knew I was falling apart; everything was caving in on me. I was staring at the ceiling, and I yelled out to God. 'I've had it. Something's got to happen, or I'm done. I'm out of here."

Tom's life would be forever changed beginning with that night. Did he immediately become the dynamic and charismatic pastor known and loved by the many people who came into his path? No, God had begun His work in Tom's life many years before, and He was showing up in the times that Tom's faith would be tested. The foundation had been laid in Tom's life from an early age; his mother and grandmother instrumental in making certain that Tom knew who God was and how important faith in his Savior would be for his life.

CHAPTER ONE
Maryland

Tom Halliburton served his country in the Air Force, first in Whiteman Air Force Base in Knob Noster, Missouri, and then in London, England. Tom and his wife, Lois, moved to Maryland in 1969, with Tom receiving a honorable discharge for his military service. While attending college classes at the University of Maryland to obtain his degree, Tom served in uniform with the Montgomery County Police Department for a short time before transitioning to an assignment working undercover. The location placed him near Washington, DC. Trained by the CIA and working primarily to take drugs off the streets, Tom dressed the part, wearing his hair long with a beard. Driving a yellow and black Chevy Nova, 'four on the floor,' Tom was ready. Signing up to work undercover wasn't a hard choice; he told his boss that he considered pulling someone over on the side of the road more dangerous than working undercover. Tom didn't just work undercover – he lived undercover, never leaving the character behind. Most of his work was done at night, on the midnight shift. His nickname was 'Animal.' Why? Because almost everyone thought he was crazy, and he worked to uphold that reputation. It helped him to become the good undercover cop that he was.

It wasn't a great job for a married man. Tom was gone most of the time at night, and Jason, his oldest son, was born in 1973. The struggles were real, just as they are for all newly married couples and new parents. They were even more so because of Tom's placement undercover, thus, beginning the first of many struggles of married life.

Tom had an informant who went by the names Crime Wave and Jimmy Piece. While many thought that Tom was crazy – a reputation he pursued – Jimmy McClain, aka Jimmy Piece, aka Crime Wave, was really wild. Nobody wanted to mess with him. The Maryland State Troopers had been after him for a long time, primarily because he was an expert at ripping them off. An undercover cop would pose as someone who wanted to buy drugs, and Jimmy could sniff them out. He would pose as a drug dealer, take their money to go and buy drugs, and then split with the money. As Tom explained it, Jimmy felt that anybody stupid enough to give the money up front to a drug dealer to get the drugs must be undercover. Eventually, Jimmy was arrested, and Tom's boss called all the cops in the unit together and told them that someone needed to work with this guy; he would be a great informant. It was going to be hard to convince anyone to take Jimmy on as an informant, but Tom was up to the task. Threatening Jimmy with his life, he told him, *"I'll turn you from a well-adjusted heroin user to a mal-adjusted drunk."* Jimmy responded with, "Well, that's better than going to jail." And a successful partnership of sorts was formed. Working together for much of the time that Tom was in Maryland, many drug dealers were taken off the streets.

'Animal' (Tom) and 'Crime Wave' (Jimmy McClain) became well-known in the area. No one wanted to mess with them, and even though someone might suspect something was amiss about a drug deal, they didn't wish to draw the attention of Animal or Crime Wave. Tom and Jimmy McClain were successful in bringing down some of the big drug dealers in the area.

Opportunities arose to shut down some even bigger fish, but circumstances intervened to stop the investigation. Tom remembers observing a plane that had been claimed to be bringing in large shipments of marijuana to sell. When the higher-ups were notified, Tom's part of the operation was complete. When he questioned what was happening, he was told that the plane belonged to a prominent lawyer in DC. Ironically, communication ceased.

Working undercover did, indeed, reveal some of the worst drug dealers. Seldom arresting anyone for possession of marijuana, those dealers were avenues into the world of harder drugs.

One of the largest drug busts occurred in an industrial complex. The department knew that someone was selling large quantities of PCP and sending it out across the country. It was up to Tom and his unit to find the person responsible. Tom had an idea that he knew could either play out well, or end up letting the dealer know that they were looking for him. Putting his trust in the local UPS guy, he tells him about the PCP distribution. He asks him to contact him if he sees anything during his rounds as a deliveryman that might be interesting to the police department.

A few days later, the UPS man called the office and asked for Tom by name. He said that he was at a company warehouse and that another guy was running a lab there. Finding the drug dealer unconscious, the

UPS guy was going to call for help, but he called Tom first. Tom was at the scene within a short time and spotted a huge, round tub full of the chemical known as PCP. Tom called the Bureau of Narcotics and Dangerous Drugs (now called the DEA) and reported the find. The Bureau arrived quickly and said that the lab in the warehouse was better than their own lab. They took over the investigation. Tom didn't care that they did; it meant he didn't have to do the paperwork. Tom, however, was the arresting officer, so he was interested in finding out more.

The facts revealed that the arrested man was the son of someone high-up in the medical field in Washington, DC. The investigation showed that two years earlier, the drug dealer was run over by a city bus and ended up with a serious problem with prescription drugs. When he could no longer get his pain medication from his doctor, he began making his own, increased his volume, and began selling it. He lived in an affluent part of DC, a section known as Chevy Chase, in a beautiful home, where the DEA found a multitude of guns.

Interestingly, the investigation revealed that the operation was likely a one-man job and that, as the defendant was making the concoction, he breathed in the PCP and passed out. Before he was tried in court for the production and distribution of the PCP, he committed suicide.

Tom and his unit were involved in many encounters with dealers that were distributing large quantities of illegal drugs, both prescription and otherwise, during his time working undercover in Maryland.

"I never had any regrets about working undercover. I enjoyed most of it. Yeah, the bad times were bad. Even with all that, I was never really afraid. I probably should have been; that's been a problem most of my life. But I was good at undercover."

Bars were a popular place for drug deals and opportunities to find out about deals that would be going down. One bar in particular stood out in Tom's memories of his Maryland undercover work. Hanging out there often, he knew many of the waitresses. As is always the case in drug-dealer-frequented bars, some of the patrons would become obnoxious or simply rowdy in their behavior, particularly in their interactions with the waitresses. One young man, usually drunk, was often inconsiderate of the waitresses and harassed them regularly, repeatedly telling one waitress to come over and sit in his lap. Tom had finally witnessed enough of the behavior, stood, and told the man to leave her alone. The young man, not aware of who he was messing with, replied, "Who's gonna make me?" Tom didn't waste any time. He told him that he would make him, and hit him. He hit him quite hard, and the young man got up and left. As far as Tom is aware, he never came back. Tom wasn't worried about repercussions; he figured that it would help his image on the job.

Unfortunately, a bond had then been formed between Tom and the waitress. Her boyfriend, soon to be her husband, was appreciative of Tom taking up for his fiancée. When the waitress tells Tom that her boyfriend wants him to come to their wedding, and that her boyfriend has got drugs coming in from California for the event, Tom realizes that there is a problem. Assuring the waitress that he would be there, Tom had no intention of going to the wedding or ever going back into the bar again. At headquarters, he tells his Major what was going on and what was going to happen. He told him that he couldn't do it. He had, against his intentions, formed a relationship with the waitress and her fiancé, and it would be difficult for him to go and make an arrest. At that point, Tom is absolved of any responsibility, and it is up to the Major what happens next. Walking away from that incident, Tom is unaware of what transpired at the wedding.

Tom's partner, Micky Conboy, became a close friend. Tom and Micky spent a lot of time working together and drinking together. Their conversations would become serious at times, and although Tom didn't share his faith with Micky as he would with others in later years, Micky did broach the subject.

Spending one afternoon drinking and planning a drug bust that was a couple of weeks away, Micky asked Tom if he believed in God. Tom answered him that he indeed believed in God.

Micky, fidgeting and then draining his beer, had sighed. "So, where do you think God is, Tom?"

Tom recalls hesitating for just a moment. The bars they hung out in, the undercover work, the places and people they had to interact with to pursue the worst of the drug dealers in the Maryland/DC area, those places didn't proclaim God's existence. Tom replied, "*Well, I know where He's not. He's not here in DC.*"

Micky nodded. "Yeah, okay. Well, after we make this deal, after we get these guys, why don't we go where you would be comfortable, you know, where God might be?"

Tom didn't hesitate this time. "*I know God is in Tennessee.*"

Author's Note:
Knowing Tom as well as I do, I can attest that Tom believes that God is, indeed, everywhere as Proverbs 15:3 says: "The eyes of the Lord are in every place, keeping watch on the evil and the good." (ESV). Tom, whether aware of it or subconsciously, knew that God was calling him to Tennessee, where the seed of his faith had been sown as a child.

Washington, DC, was practically across the street from Tom and Micky's work area, and the main drag running into DC was Georgia Avenue, where the drug deal they had been planning would take place at the Holiday Inn. Micky and Jim Evans[1] would be the buyers of a cocaine deal worth seventeen thousand dollars, a considerable amount in the 1970s. Cocaine was becoming a hot item in DC, a rich man's drug. Tom was too well-known in the area and might be recognized by the drug dealers, so he could not be in the room with Micky. He would be in the room adjacent to the drug deal, out of sight. Tom and several other officers would be monitoring the conversation in the room where the drug transaction would take place, using microphones placed in strategic areas. Micky, playing his part, had a test kit to ensure that the cocaine was good. The signal

---

[1] Name changed.

would be for Micky to say that the cocaine tested good, and then Tom and the other officers would go in.

Everything was going as planned until Micky gave the signal, and Tom, along with the other officers in the adjacent room, opened the door separating them. Shots were fired by the drug dealers, one hitting Jim Evans in the shoulder, and another hitting Micky in the back as he was coming toward the door. Micky fell on the floor in the hallway. Tom, uncertain of his partner's condition, returned fire with the two criminals. Dodging gunfire and trying to get to his partner, Tom was fortunate that he wasn't also shot during the exchange. Another officer shot both assailants and they were down. Calls were made for back-up and assistance from medical personnel.

Tom reached his partner and held him. Micky looked up at Tom and said, "T, I got gut-shot." Those were the last words he spoke to Tom, while Tom continued to hold him and pray. Tom prayed and performed CPR. Despite CPR and heroic attempts by the paramedics, Micky died at the hospital.

Pain and loss consume one's thoughts when faced with such horror, and Tom was no different. His friend, his partner, a man with a wife and daughter, a good cop. Tom couldn't save him, and the realization that Micky was now in God's hands didn't come to him automatically. Instead, it was anger, Tom's old friend, that surfaced. Loss and anger, in the face of evil, are sometimes the shield we choose. Tom soon found out that his constant shield against evil was his God, always present. The day was coming for a reckoning.

The investigation revealed that the two men, both of whom were deceased when they reached the hospital, had been operating in the same way for quite some time. Setting people up for a drug sale, then taking both the money and drugs and leaving the buyers dead, the two criminals were both students at the University of Maryland.

Washington, DC and the surrounding area experienced a massive surge in heroin use and addiction in the early 1970s. Jumping from roughly 5000 addicts in January of 1970 to over 18,000 by the end of the year, the drug problem was on everyone's radar. Many community organizations and government programs worked to curtail the issue, but were overwhelmed by the sheer numbers. Cocaine gained popularity among the rich, primarily because of its high cost and the idea that it was a special drug.

Undercover work has existed for many years, the earliest dating back to the early 19th century. Now prevalent in both law enforcement and journalism, the 1960s and 1970s saw significant increases in both, primarily due to growing needs in these fields. However, the times when officers were put 'on leave' for an extended period when there was a shooting, specifically an officer who was injured or killed, were in the future. The early 1970s had not recognized the need for such a lapse in working hours. Two days after his partner was murdered, Tom was back on the job, buying drugs.

"*I never didn't believe in God,*" Tom said. "*I struggled with things and questioned them, but I never didn't believe. When my partner was killed, it was a blank time in my life, a black period.*"

William Patrick (Micky) Conboy, Jr., Tom's partner, died on December 29th of 1973, when Tom was only a few months away from graduating from the University of Maryland, with degrees in Law Enforcement and English. Tom's son, Jason, was approaching his first birthday in a few months, and Tom told his commanding officer that he was going to move to Tennessee. The conversation he had with his partner, Micky, was never far away from his thoughts. God was in Tennessee, and Tom knew that he was supposed to go there. Tom's boss just laughed and said, "Don't you go down there and get religious on me."

Tom knew it was the right thing to do: leave and go to Tennessee. Still thinking about his partner's murder, he wanted to return to Nashville. Micky's death haunted Tom. He thought about dying.

"I wanted to be buried at Spring Hill Cemetery, like all good East Nashville boys wanted."

Tom undercover.

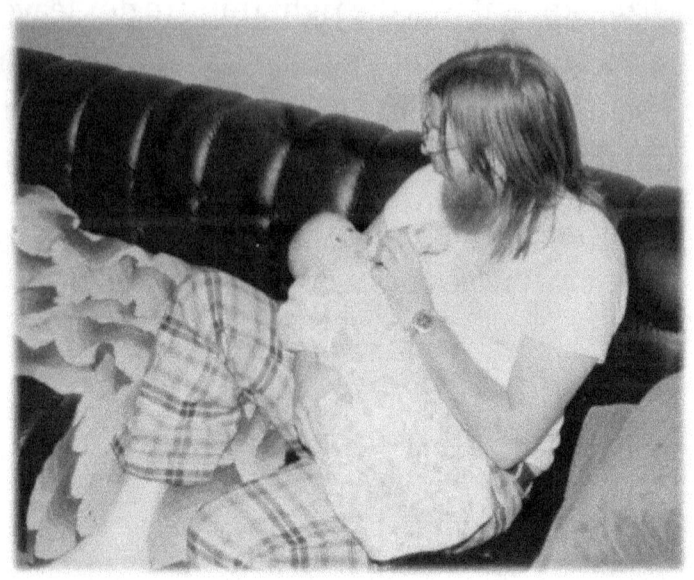

Tom at home while working undercover, feeding Jason.

Official Report:

Private William Patrick Conboy, Jr.

Montgomery County Police Department, Maryland

End of Watch: Saturday, December 29, 1973

William Patrick Conboy, Jr. Private William Conboy was shot and killed during an undercover narcotics operation at a hotel at 8777 Georgia Avenue in Silver Spring. He and another undercover officer had met the two suspects in a hotel lobby where they were patted down before being taken to the suspects' room on the 10th floor. Instead of the anticipated cocaine purchase, one of the suspects drew a handgun and shot Private Conboy in the back. Backup officers immediately entered the room and fatally shot one of the suspects. Private Conboy was a U.S. Marine Corps veteran and had served with the Montgomery County Police Department for three years. He was survived by his wife and 2-year-old daughter.

Record Details:	Incident Details:
Age: 25	Cause: Gunfire / Handgun
Tour: 3 years	Offender:
Military Veteran	One shot and killed undercover

CHAPTER TWO
Tennessee

Tom had a relative who worked for the Gallatin Sheriff's Department who helped him get a job with Sumner County. Making a home in Madison, Tennessee, with Lois, his first wife, and Jason, who had turned one, Tom was undercover for the Hendersonville Police Department, a few miles away. Also close by was the area where Tom grew up and attended Isaac Litton High School. If anyone should run into Tom while he was working undercover, they wouldn't have been surprised to think that he was into drugs. A wild child in school, Tom was frequently in trouble. There was little concern about his cover being blown.

Aggressively driving around in a yellow and black Dodge Charger, Tom looked the part. Undercover work in Hendersonville, Tennessee, differed significantly from his experiences in Maryland and DC. Most of the work centered around wannabe gang members and marijuana.

Many of the young men who were involved in illegal drugs and gang activity were sentenced to the Turney Center in Only, Tennessee, a facility in Hickman County. The center was named after Governor Turney, who had advocated for the rehabilitation of inmates and the separation of youth from adult criminals. The facility provided education and skills to prepare the young men for life after they had served their sentence. One of the skills offered prepared young men for work as mechanics, and police department employees could have their cars repaired there for free.

Tom knew the Warden, Jim Rose, and Tom took his Charger to Turney to have some work done. Standing outside with Tom, Warden Rose asked Tom if he recognized the guy working on his car. When Tom replied that he didn't know him, the Warden said that the young man had said Tom was the one who put him in prison. Tom took a second look.

"*I recognized him then. Yeah, I had bought drugs from him and then busted him. I asked the Warden if I needed to worry about my car, and he said no. He said, 'That boy's not going to hurt your car. We're watching him.' He's right. The kid didn't hurt my car."*

Tom had been working nights undercover for most of his married life. Finally receiving the opportunity to work as a probation and parole officer in Nashville, he jumped at the chance. He wasn't undercover any longer, and he was making more money. That position led to a promotion, and he was named the State Director for the Model X Offender program. A program established to assist offenders in reintegrating into society after their release, it was funded by the federal government. The program offered services, including temporary housing, job training, and family support. Tom had twelve employees working for him in different parts of the State. Travelling throughout Tennessee, Tom once again found himself away from home much of the time.

As many federal government programs do, the money ran out. Tom was faced with twelve people whom he had instructed and worked with who would soon be out of a job. He wasn't concerned about his career; he had been a parole and probation officer before, and could return to it. However, the men working for him might not be so lucky. Frustration and anger, combined with a drinking problem, caused a deep depression in Tom.

Finally, successfully finding positions for all of the people working for him – and many in the corrections department – Tom returned to working as a probation officer. Unfortunately, things continued in a downhill spiral.

Lois was working for a law firm downtown, and when Tom was working undercover, they didn't see each other often. As Tom stated, *"We would just pass by each other sometimes."* With Tom's new hours, he could see that the marriage was truly failing. He and Lois didn't argue; they were indifferent to one another. Mitchell was born in 1978. Two boys at home, and Tom tried his best to spend as much time as he could with them, taking Jason fishing often. As Tom revealed the depths of pain he was in during that period, the depression was evident.

"I was miserable; she was miserable. I was falling apart. The only good thing I did right during that time was being a father. I worked hard at that."

Tom's drinking increased. Every day at 11:30, he would go to lunch and drink beer, believing it would help him get through the day. Never missing a day of work or a deadline, Tom continued to do his job, and do it well, but he felt he needed that drink to keep going.

Weekends, when Tom wasn't taking Jason fishing, were all spent the same way. Friday night would begin with Tom hooking up his boat and driving to Priest Lake to fish, sometimes fishing and drinking all night. Then, after eating breakfast at the Waffle House, Tom would head up to Kentucky Lake with the boat. Sometimes he would stop and pick up a friend, someone he worked with, and they would fish all day. Driving back home late Saturday night, Tom would stop two or three times to get a beer on the way. The following weekend, he would do it all over again.

Tom can look back and see the demons at work in his life, trying to destroy his faith. His words were haunting, his remembrance of the depths of despair.

"There was so much that I couldn't let go of. My partner getting killed, and just everything else. I crashed and burned. Everything came falling down. It all just seemed like it was going to hell.

The time came when I knew I was falling apart; everything was caving in on me. I was staring at the ceiling, and I yelled out to God. 'I've had it. Something's got to happen, or I'm done. I'm out of here.' I prayed that night. I said, 'God, if You are there and You are the God that my mother and my grandmother taught me about, if You put love back into my life, into my heart, I'll follow You anywhere. I'll do whatever You ask me to do."

God made his presence known to Tom at that moment, in a big way.

"*I had a Damascus Road experience; many have a rocking chair experience. You get to the same place either way. A rocking chair experience with Jesus, you follow Him because you've always followed Him. You don't know any other way. Mine was down on my knees at my wits' end. I was desperate.*"

— Tom

CHAPTER THREE
Revelation

"BANG. It happened. All of the issues I had been dealing with: the problems, the fear, the anger. It was gone."

The significance of this profound event elevated his enthusiasm for Jesus, even though Tom didn't receive the reaction he wanted from his wife. He immediately went upstairs and woke her. He told Lois that he had just experienced a moment with God and that God had put love back into his life and his heart. Lois didn't understand and was not moved by the exposure of his innermost feelings. Even though the woman by his side didn't share in his jubilation, Tom slept well and arose the next morning to go back downstairs and began praying.

Praying on the way to work, upon his arrival, he told his secretary that he needed to close the door to his office and couldn't be interrupted for a short time. This was a new occurrence, and he could tell his secretary was disturbed. Tom told her that something had happened the night before, and he needed to work his way through it. It was nine o'clock in the morning.

"I prayed some more. I asked for forgiveness, pouring out everything inside me. I wanted to understand what had happened to me. The words tumbled out, making no sense to anyone but God. And then, whatever 'IT' was, it was inside me. I began talking, talking in a language I didn't understand. A new, a different experience for me. I had no background in speaking like this. I didn't understand it. But oh, it felt so good. I knew. It was the Holy Spirit."

Tom remained in his office for over an hour.

Author's Note:
Tom told me about this experience several times during our talks. It was so imprinted upon his spirit that he repeated this event, often in the same words, each time. The emotional upheaval in his soul, the joy and truth were both zealous and undeniable.

His secretary, still a bit concerned, wondered about the language she heard coming from inside Tom's office door, and was thankful when he emerged from his office with a smile and headed down the hall. "*I need to talk to Byron Dumas,*" he said.

A parole officer, Byron Dumas, was also a part-time Pentecostal minister. Tom told him what had happened to him, both the night before and a few minutes earlier in his office. Although Tom knew about speaking in tongues from the Bible lessons he had grown up with, he had not experienced it on a personal, spiritual level.

"*Well, does that happen to Methodists?*" Tom asked Byron.

Byron replied, "Not that I've ever heard of."

The Pentecostal minister gave Tom two books, *Nine O'clock in the Morning* by Dennis Bennett and *The Partakers* by Bob Tuttle. While Tom heartily recommends both books, one of them holds special significance for him. Tom's experience of receiving the Holy Spirit came at the nine o'clock hour, and the Episcopal priest, Dennis Bennett, had a similar experience.

God was working in so many ways. Tom, at the time of his spiritual awakening, or revelation, was working with the DUI court as a senior probation officer. With a caseload of over one hundred people, he had court on Fridays and would spend the morning hearing from those who had violated parole or probation. The court cases were over around eleven, and it was time for lunch.

Byron Dumas told Tom about the Full Gospel Businessmen's Luncheon, held every Friday at various restaurants in Nashville hotels. Tom remembers the first luncheon he attended at a Best Western restaurant. As he walked into the hotel, another man was in front of him, going to the same luncheon. Several other men are standing across the room at a bar, drunk and staggering around. The man in front of Tom nodded at them and said, "There, but by the grace of God, go I," and asked Tom if he was attending the luncheon.

Tom remembers many of the men who were there that day, and that he continued to see at luncheons across the Nashville area. Joe Morgan, Wade Joyner, Bill Wade. Wade Joyner gave his testimony that day, and Tom credits him with being *"one of the kindest and gentlest people I've ever known in my life and one of the most dedicated Christians."*

Tom met and became close to many of the attendees. F. B. Ferrier, Paul Gupton, Don Finto – a preacher at Belmont, and an associate at McKendree Methodist, are only a few men with whom Tom studied the Bible. The luncheons continued, and Tom attended every one that he could. He heard them talking about their relationship with the Lord and saw that they were not inspired just on Sunday, but every day of their lives. These men are witnessing about Jesus to everybody they come in contact with, each in their own way. Tom feels God leading him to something; he's involved with the luncheons and going to Bible studies.

F. B. Ferrier had a Bible study in his home on Thursday nights. There were sometimes thirty to forty people there. *"I began giving my testimony, telling what had happened to me and what had led me there. I talked about my partner's death and how the Lord spoke to me."*

Tom became involved in several different charismatic churches. In these churches, the Holy Spirit was moving, and Tom could learn more about his experiences and what God was telling him to do.

God was still working on Tom; despite the incredible revelation that he experienced, Tom was still doing many of the same things that had led him to desperation.

Tom had a friend, a drinking buddy, Billy Sands[1]. They would see each other from time to time. Both were members of the Veterans of Foreign Wars, and they would pick different places to go out drinking. One of their final nights together is imprinted upon Tom's memory. Billy said, "I know what happened. I know that you're a Christian now, and I guess that's good. But I don't see anything different about you. You still fight; you still drink. You still have a reputation at the Legion, and you know, I don't want to be around you now. I really don't, Tom." Billy left.

God had taken a friend, someone close to Tom, and used that man to get Tom to listen to God more closely. Tom prayed and asked God to heal him, and asked that his only addiction be for the Lord. Tom didn't take another drink for years, and then only occasionally, never in need. He lost a close friend that night, and although they had a few more conversations, they didn't resume their close friendship. One of the few social activities he had was gone, and his entire social life revolved around Bible study.

"I'm like a sponge all the time, every place I go, everything I see and hear. It was the Lord; He was everywhere, and I wanted to be there. People listened to my

---

[1] Name changed.

testimony, mainly because it was a significant life change. I had been locked up in a London jail; I was a narc working undercover; I lost my partner in a drug shootout; and then a miracle happened. I thought I was doing what God wanted me to do. But I did have this feeling that something was missing."

Byron Dumas headed up a new group called the New Wine Ministry, a group of young Christians at Vanderbilt meeting at the Episcopal Church. With a growing reputation as a gifted speaker, Tom began attending the group and became heavily involved. Prayer was a primary component of the group, and prayer was centered around healing for those who were sick. Miracles are happening, and Tom's understanding of what it means to be a believer is growing.

Tom was busy; he liked his job, and his faith was growing stronger by the day. But his marriage continued to struggle. Tom and Lois were okay financially; their jobs were interesting and paid a decent wage. Lois would occasionally attend church on Sundays, but never really committed to it. They socialized with Byron and his wife a few times, but Lois was against a more permanent relationship with them or the church.

"I don't blame her for that. Everyone has a different walk with God. I've lived long enough to realize it. Our lives weren't working together. Stuff happens. It just does."

Change comes sometimes when we least expect it, and opportunities arise from places unforeseen. A move to Florida was not expected or desired, at least by Tom. But God has a way of working for His purpose wherever we are.

CHAPTER FOUR
Florida

Tom was involved in several churches in Nashville and the surrounding area. Heavily involved with the New Wine program at Vanderbilt, Tom felt led into a healing ministry. Observing and being a part of miraculous healings moved Tom to a deeper walk with the Lord, and he welcomed each new experience with an open heart.

Leaving Nashville had not been on Tom's mind, but he, by his own admission, had never turned away from what he termed 'an adventure.' The marriage was in shambles, but Tom sensed hope when Lois said that her grandmother wanted to give them a house in Jacksonville, Florida. Although Tom and Lois enjoyed a home located in a nice neighborhood in Antioch, Tennessee, the lure of a free home enticed them both.

They discussed it, and thought about it for a few months, Tom praying about the move and the possibilities that it would entail. Could this be a second chance at their marriage? Two young boys were the primary concern. Lois wanted to go; she urged Tom to agree.

The Antioch home was put up for sale, and Tom gave his notice at work. He wasn't concerned about obtaining a job in Florida. With connections through the Full Gospel Businessmen's group in Nashville, he felt confident that he would find the right position quickly.

Their house in Antioch sold within a few weeks; profits from the sale, Tom's retirement fund from the State of Tennessee, plus savings in the bank, gave Tom and Lois a good start in Florida, especially considering that they would not be purchasing a home. Finding a job soon would assure that the money remained in the bank, and Tom was hopeful. A friend, Philip Grant[1], in Jacksonville, had told him that he had the best job in the world for him, and it would be ready for him.

As soon as they arrived in Jacksonville, Tom called Philip and went to his house to discuss the new job. Philip gave him a book and told him to read it, also

---

[1] Name changed.

admonishing, "If you don't see Jesus all over this, you can come to my driveway and throw this book at me."

Tom read the book, but it wasn't quite what he expected. The book was a recruiting tool used by Amway to procure salespeople for their product line. Tom was not interested in selling Amway and was aware that the company had its problems. Even if it had been a company above reproach, Tom knew that his place was not to be working for them. He didn't know the plans God had for him, but he felt certain that Amway[1] was not it.

Tom called Philip and asked him to come over. As soon as he pulled up in the driveway, Tom walked out and threw the book at him. Philip laughed, but Tom's relationship and contact with the Jacksonville area's Full Gospel Men's group disappeared. His connection was gone.

Tom began working as a claims adjuster for Nationwide Insurance Company, the first of several diverse positions he held while in Florida. He had a company car with Nationwide, and the job paid well.

---

[1] According to Wikipedia, the Federal Trade Commission (FTC) investigated Amway in 1979 and determined that it was not a pyramid scheme, but ordered the company to stop engaging in certain practices.

Tom was eager to become involved in a church and immediately began looking for a church home. He recalled one Sunday morning when he pulled into the parking lot of a church that he had heard had an exceptional preacher, well known in the area. As Tom pulled into the parking lot, something told him that this was not where God wanted him to be. A sign was in front of Tom's car. 'Pastors Parking Only/Violators Will Be Towed.' That sign gave off a vibe that Tom didn't feel good about; it wasn't the kind of sign that should be at a church.

"I found another Full Gospel Business group and became really involved with them, and with churches in the area that were charismatic. Once I had volunteered to give my testimony, word spread, and I gave testimony at several churches in the area."

Tom's job was going well; he was finding his way into the groups that God called him to. However, his marriage was failing, bitterly. He prayed for an answer; he begged Lois to join him in Bible study groups. He had thought that once they were in Florida, she would become involved. She had attended a few in Nashville, but she didn't want anything to do with it in Florida.

Tom and Lois had been married for over nine years. He had been introduced to Lois by her mother, who was in an English class with Tom when he was stationed in London (The University of Maryland offered extension classes to servicemen at the London AFB). Lois' father was a Navy commander also stationed there, and shortly after Tom and Lois were engaged, Lois' father was transferred to Bethesda, Maryland. Tom and Lois traveled to Bethesda for their wedding, and after completing his service in London, Tom and Lois moved back to Maryland, where he continued his studies and became an undercover officer with the Montgomery County Police Department.

Their first son, Jason, was born in 1973 in Maryland; Tom's partner, Micky Conboy, was murdered in December of 1973; and after moving to Nashville, Mitchell was born in May of 1978. Travels, births, and a traumatic death had rocked them, but Tom was praying for reconciliation, for something to happen, for the marriage to succeed.

Nationwide Insurance Company required its employees, and particularly their adjustors, to attend training in Columbus, Ohio, twice a year. It was generally a constructive, professional conference, and Tom enjoyed the programs and the people he met there. The conferences were not very long, but required several overnight stays, and Tom would fly back and forth from Florida to Ohio.

Tom returned home from his third conference and went straight to the office from the airport. During his lunch break, Tom went home to eat, expecting Lois to be there. She was not, but she called him on the phone. "Tom, I want you to leave," she said. She continued by telling him that it was her house – there were never any legal papers signed that he was aware of – and that she had the right to make him leave.

"I was shocked. I knew I wasn't the best husband in the world, but I was always faithful. We have these two boys, and Mitchell is still in diapers, while Jason is around seven years old. I'm not sure if Lois planned it that way, to move and then be done with me. I guess I took some clothes with me. I don't remember a lot. I went to a hotel. I had a little money with me. I went to the bank the next day to withdraw some money, and the teller recognized me. She said, 'Tom, I'm sorry. Lois cleared out the account. There is not any money in there.' Again, I was shocked. It was thousands of dollars. The money from the sale of the house, my pension checks, all of it. Gone. I had nothing and had to start over from scratch. I felt lucky that I had a company car."

Tom was caught blind-sided. He wasn't aware that things had deteriorated as much as they had, still hopeful that things could be worked out. It was not to be. Lawyers worked out the details, and there was only one time when Tom and Lois were both in the same room. Tom's lawyer told Lois that Tom didn't want a divorce, but she was adamant. There was no going back. Legally, Lois didn't do anything wrong in taking the money; Tom could have done the same since both names were on the account. Tom told Lois at the final meeting that he never would have done that to her, taken all the money. He said he might have taken some of it, but not all of it, and that he probably would have turned it all over to her if she had asked.

Tom lived with a friend, Chris Regas, for a few days while he looked for a place to live. God's presence revealed itself once again. An ad was in the paper; a man, Wade Hopkins[1], was looking for a Christian roommate. Hopkins had served a stint in the Navy and was considering going back in. Meanwhile, he needed a roommate. It wasn't a large place, but it was big enough for Tom to bring the boys there, and Wade didn't mind having Jason and Mitchell visit.

Tom had unlimited visitation rights with the boys and had no issues with paying the child support agreed upon. He loved his boys, and being a good father was important to him. Tom's first visit with the boys was a long time coming. During the divorce proceedings, he

---

[1] Name changed.

had only been allowed to talk to the boys a few times on the phone. Finally, Lois agreed for Tom to pick up the boys at the daycare center for the weekend. That weekend turned into three months.

Tom was working, the boys were in daycare, and since Wade had decided to rejoin the Navy, Tom began looking for a place to live. Finding a trailer with a big yard was the perfect answer. The boys could play outside. Tom struggled, but got by. With a good job and a company car, he could scrape by and pay his child support and other expenses.

Tom started visiting different churches, seeking the same type of atmosphere he had found in Nashville. He missed what he had there, but his boys live in Florida and Tom was going to stay near his boys. They needed him. Continuing to give his testimony and witnessing as he felt God wanted him to do, Tom still didn't find the church he wanted to call home.

God used a sweet little old lady to lead Tom to his next church home.

Insurance guys talk to each other often, first about business and then become friends with common goals. A friend of Tom's who worked with another insurance company asked Tom, as a claims adjustor, to talk to this sweet lady about some stuff that had been stolen from her.

What began as an interview about her stolen jewelry became a testimony. Tom told her about his walk with the Lord and his life. She was intrigued and asked him to come to her church. She attended a Methodist church, and Tom told her that he had been a Methodist, raised in a Methodist church, and he would come.

Tom attended that church the following Sunday, walking in and sitting on the side with the fewest people, by himself. Bill Caldwell, the pastor of the church, distributed a form to everyone. The form gave opportunities for volunteer work, and Pastor Caldwell requested everyone fill it out and mention any interests. Tom filled out the form, noting that he would like to work with the youth, and put the form in the offering plate when it came around.

Tom couldn't wait for a phone call or more conversation at church. He decided that he needed to talk to the preacher in person and discuss what he would like to do. Unbeknownst to Tom, the sweet little old lady had already spoken to Pastor Caldwell, telling him everything she had learned when Tom had visited her.

Tom walked into the pastor's office, and Bill Caldwell said, "You're Tom Halliburton." Tom replied that he was, and Caldwell continued. "I'm not interested in what you want to do. I need to tell you what you're going to do."

Tom was taken aback, but he knew that God was at work here. "*Well, okay,*" he said.

Tom learned that the youth group was small, with only six or seven attendees. However, the Sunday School class for adults was large and needed a teacher. The previous teacher was leaving, and Bill Caldwell decided that he had found his new teacher. He told Tom that he would be the new youth director and also the new Sunday School teacher for the adult class.

Heavily involved over the next several months, Tom loved everything he was doing there. Joining the church, Tom had connected with the youth and increased their attendance to between fifteen and twenty. Also teaching the oldest members of the congregation, Tom saw great things happening in the church. God was moving through the hearts and souls of the members and blessing Tom with fellowship with other Christians.

Divorce weighed heavily on Tom, and God provided Tom with other Christians who helped him through the haze and onto a more productive, happier existence. Sharing his testimony and the pain of losing his partner during a drug bust in Maryland brought him closer to those who needed to hear the story of triumph over tragedy, of trust in the Lord over doubt.

Church ladies are a well-known asset to the single man. Always on the lookout for the perfect match, the church ladies of Cedar Crest Methodist Church were no different, and they were sure that they could find the right woman for Tom. Despite their best efforts, however, Tom managed to avoid the 'casserole crowd' as he named them.

It had been over a year since Tom's divorce, and Pastor Bill Caldwell decided that the time had come for Tom to begin dating. When Caldwell told Tom that he had arranged a date for him for the church Christmas party, Tom responded that the last thing he needed was a date. Gun-shy after his divorce, Tom didn't feel ready to think about dating. But Bill Caldwell wouldn't take no for an answer. God was at work in Tom's life. He just didn't recognize that God was involved in all aspects of his life.

CHAPTER FIVE
Florida & Gayle

Gayle Black was not particularly gun-shy, but she also was not in a hurry to begin a new relationship. Navigating motherhood as a single parent and working full-time in a salon as a beautician, she had her hands full. Her ex-husband had been an alcoholic and had no connection with his children when he died. Julie was twelve years old, and David was only four. Gayle had no desire to jump into a relationship with anyone, much less someone with a lot of baggage. And Tom Halliburton had some baggage.

Gayle attended Cedar Crest Methodist Church regularly, singing in the choir and enjoying a good relationship with many of the members. When she was approached about having a 'blind' date with Tom Halliburton, she agreed. She had seen him in church, had heard others talk about him, and knew that he was hungry for a closer walk with God. One date would go a long way in letting her know if they would enjoy each other's company.

Gayle knew he had two children, two boys who were with him most of the time. Well-behaved children, and that meant a lot. He was divorced, and Gayle figured that she would, at some point, if they ventured into serious conversations, find out why he was divorced.

There was something else Gayle had noticed about Tom Halliburton, although she couldn't put her finger on precisely what it was. Gayle was a Christian who took her faith seriously and talked with her Lord often. Did He put that something in her mind? When Gayle had been in her teens, she remembered how certain she had been that she would marry a preacher. Tom wasn't a preacher, but he was certainly sharing his testimony with many people and reaching so many of them with his story.

The church Christmas party would be the perfect first date. Plenty of people around, both of them knew most of the people that would be there well, and there would be no pressure, or so Gayle thought.

The night of the Christmas party arrived, and Gayle took extra care to get ready. This was special, she could feel it. Arriving at the party, she expected Tom to be there already, but he had not yet entered the room. However, when he did, he sat down, but not close to Gayle. Tom was saying very little, eating from the snacks brought by the church ladies, and making small talk with anyone who came by him.

Finally, unable to ignore the stares and shrugs she received from friends noticing her discomfort, she approached Tom. He was rising from his chair as she walked up and sat down next to him. "Excuse me, Tom. You're hurting my feelings. Everyone here knows that you're supposed to be here with me. You and I are supposed to be having a date."

It was the best thing that could have happened. Tom told her that he was preparing to come and sit beside her, and that he was sorry he had been acting the way he had. He told her how pretty she looked, which broke the ice. An easier conversation followed; when they left the party, they continued their date at Denny's restaurant, and found that they did have a lot in common and could potentially enjoy each other's company. Both in their 30s, both with children at home, Gayle and Tom realized a shared love for the Lord, which brought them closer together.

Gayle was an open book about her life before Tom, and told him everything. Tom, however, was more selective. Perhaps he didn't want to scare her away. She had heard his testimony; she knew about his children and his divorce. She knew he loved God and tried to follow Him and would work feverishly for the Lord. She didn't learn about his other life, his undercover work, until after they had been seeing one another for a few months. By that time, Tom's revelation didn't deter her. She loved him.

Their dates were simple, usually spent at Tom's home. Gayle would bring Julie and David. The four children got to know one another. Julie and Jason became very close and remained so. David and Mitchell were very young, but played together well. There were a few movie dates, taking the children to a special showing at the drive-in theater. The talks between Gayle and Tom would last deep into the night, heart to heart.

Gayle knew she loved him, and Tom made it clear he felt the same. *"I fell in love. Hard. Luckily, she fell in love with me, too."*

Talk of marriage came naturally. When marriage was first mentioned, Gayle told Tom that she had prayed about it and felt that she was going to marry a preacher. Tom told her that he wasn't a preacher. *"She told me that she thought I was, she thought I was headed that way, and I was kind of a preacher already."*

They wanted to spend the rest of their lives together; they loved each other's children and were eager to start their family life together. Pastor Bill Caldwell, the same man that had set up their first date, married them on April 21, 1981.

Only a few months previous, Tom had been a featured speaker at the United Methodist Men's Conference, held at a large campground near Lake Harris in Florida. Several men who had inspired Tom were going to be there, and when he was asked to give his testimony, he was both honored and blessed to attend. Bishop Max Stokes, a professor and author of *Baptism of the Holy Spirit*, was there, and Tom was excited to meet him. Tom began to recognize the effect that his testimony had on people; Tom was a man who had been, in his own words, a complete idiot, a fighter, and he had come to know the Lord.

God touched Tom again during that conference, in a special moment. Closing out the conference with all of the other speakers on Saturday night, all of the attendees were invited to come forward to talk with any speaker who had touched their heart, and many came forward. So many for both Tom and the other speakers that the conference continued until late that night. Tom was told, as he was leaving the campground, by more than one person there, that he should be going into the ministry.

The camp was a beautiful place, private and secluded. Many church retreats had been held there. Tom and Gayle's church had made arrangements for them to have their honeymoon at that camp. One of the most impactful conversations of their life would happen there.

Tom had grown tired of being a claims adjuster. Unsure of what he should be doing, he became the assistant manager at a paint and body shop. Not content there, he began selling shrimp. Meeting the boats as they came into port, he would pick out the batch of shrimp and deliver it. A friend had a truck and, in return for Tom selling his shrimp, loaned him the truck to use. Tom named the truck 'Victory at Sea.' It was seasonal work, and Tom also worked for the Pepsi company as a truck driver.

Tom and Gayle both needed the break for their honeymoon, a time to relax and talk about their future, a future that both of them felt included a ministry. Tom realized that God wanted him to take a more hands-on approach to serving Him, and Gayle was entirely on board. Tom was getting a lot of pressure from everyone to attend seminary studies. Most of the pressure, he knew, was coming from his walk with his Lord.

Tom was working all the time; he was exhausted. Selling shrimp, driving for Pepsi, working with the youth at church, a Sunday school teacher, husband, and father. It was too much. Quitting the Pepsi job didn't help as much as he thought it would. God was calling, but Tom was hesitating.

Tom talked to Gayle. Since he knew some people in Nashville, he decided to apply to a seminary close to his hometown. While Tom had lived in many places, Gayle had never lived anywhere else. She was working for Cokesbury in Jacksonville, Florida.

Gayle would go where Tom was called. "I had never seen snow. I was thirty or thirty-one years old. I was worried, but I was going wherever we needed to go."

Tom needed to throw out one more fleece, however. Tom went to talk to Bill Caldwell, his pastor. "*I had decided on Vanderbilt for seminary. It was close to my hometown, and I told Bill that if I was going into the ministry, I would get accepted for the fall semester.*" By this time, it is already May. Bill laughed and told Tom that it didn't work that way. Tom replied that he would either be accepted for the fall semester or not go. To make it even more definitive, Tom didn't send in his application until late June. The likelihood of his application even being reviewed was minuscule.

Tom realizes now that he was running away from what God wanted, and that was why he was unable to find peace.

God made it happen.

Tom and Gayle felt that Tom wouldn't be going to seminary at Vanderbilt, since he had turned in his application so late. However, two weeks before Labor Day, Tom received the phone call. School started at Vanderbilt the day after Labor Day. He had been accepted for the fall semester at Vanderbilt's seminary, and he should be there within two weeks.

"We packed up what little we had and left Jacksonville. We didn't have anywhere to live, no place to go. We had four kids and a dog we called Pepper. She was a great dog, but she bit everybody. So, maybe not so great.

So, we lived for three months at my grandfather's house, where I grew up. We were fine."

Tom was coming back to Tennessee, back to Nashville, back to Spain Avenue. Where his life and his journey had begun, where he was born into a loving,

Christian family that would influence his life in more ways than he knew.

Back to where God's plan for Tom began.

Tom & Gayle

CHAPTER SIX
1946 – 1969

"All the way through my life growing up, I was blessed to have good Sunday School teachers at the Inglewood Church. I always knew there was a God, and at least some about who Jesus was. I thought I was the luckiest kid in the world to live on Spain Avenue, go to Jere Baxter Elementary School, and then on to Litton High School. It just couldn't be any better."

The opportunity to grow up in a community that was part of a larger city and still have the experiences of a 'Mayberry' like atmosphere – that's what Nashville was back in the fifties and sixties. Family was the most important thing, and the friends that lived in your neighborhood came in second. You went to school and church with the same people you saw every day, whether it was the local Methodist, Baptist, Church of Christ, or Catholic church down on the corner. The schools were filled with kids from your street and the surrounding area. You would probably know the kids at the next school down the road; this was before neighborhood schools were dissolved and blended into the huge comprehensive schools that brought kids from all around Nashville to one building. Good or bad, it changed the dynamics of the local communities.

Thomas Halliburton, one of the first 'baby boomers,' was born February 21, 1946, at Vanderbilt Hospital, Nashville. Like many of his generation in the South, he was raised in a Christian home and lived a far simpler life than many children and young people today.

Tom had the privilege of growing up in one of those 'Mayberry-like' communities in the 1950s and 1960s, graduating from Issac Litton High School in 1964. However, his childhood was not without sorrow and change.

Tom had an older brother, Howard, who was two years older, and a younger brother, John, who was four years younger. There have been a multitude of papers written and researched about the 'middle' child, and Tom wouldn't be the exception. It's as if he came out fighting. The thing Tom remembers vividly about his childhood seems to be his realization that fighting was better than being picked on, and he learned to fight well, and often.

There was one thing Tom was afraid of, and the fear remains, a childhood memory so vivid that Tom had no hesitation in responding to the question: What are you afraid of?

"Rats. I hate rats. I'm okay with snakes and mice, you know, any of that. We had a stoker in the basement. When I was old enough, it was my job to fill up the stoker at night, and again the next morning. Shoveling the coal into the stoker, I would look over into the corner, hoping I wouldn't see it, but most of the time, there would be a rat. I still remember the way they look at you. That evil look. My grandfather called them wharf rats."

In a big, old two-story house on Spain Avenue, Tom lived in his grandparents' home for most of his childhood. There was a smaller cinderblock house, which they called the 'chicken house,' behind the house on Spain. Tom's grandfather had built the chicken house for the purpose of raising chickens and then was prohibited from doing so by the rules of the community at that time. Tom, along with his parents and older brother, lived in the chicken house for a short time while his parents were saving for a home on McGavock Pike. The Halliburton family moved to their new home on McGavock in 1950, when Tom was about four years old, but hard times were ahead. Tom's father died two years later.

Robert Howard Halliburton had survived rheumatic fever as a child, but lived with a damaged heart and valve problems. He was listed as 4F in the draft and expressed sorrow that he couldn't serve his country because of his heart problems. 4F designates a person unqualified for military service due to a medical issue. An episode with his heart led to open-heart surgery in the early 1950s. Open-heart surgery was a new and experimental field at that time, with relatively high mortality rates. Tom's father survived the surgery but died a few months later from complications.

"I remember that my father called me 'Joe Sport' and 'my Tommy Tinker.' I was so young. I remember going to the place across the street from Spring Hill Cemetery that had markers for the graves. My mother and big brother were with me. We were looking for the tombstone that would go on my daddy's grave. I looked at all those things in there and saw 'The Lord is My Shepherd' on one stone, and I told my mother that I wanted that one for my daddy. That's the one she chose."

Tom's little brother had been born while they lived on McGavock Pike; his mother now had three boys to take care of. They moved back into the house with Tom's grandparents on Spain Avenue and remained there throughout Tom's school years. Surrounded by relatives, Tom grew up in a home filled with a focus on family and church.

Ruth Halliburton had her hands full. She had two jobs: working as a cashier on weekends and as a clerk at Cokesbury during the week. Three boys at home, and thankfully, her parents could help take care of her children.

The house on Spain Avenue was a haven for Tom, important not because of what was in it, but who was in it: his mother, his grandparents, his brothers, and his aunt lived next door. His grandmother cooked large meals on Sundays, often having visitors for Sunday dinner after church. Some relatives, some friends, and many good memories.

Ruth loved to fish, or maybe she just loved going fishing. Come spring, she would tell Tom, "The red buds are blooming. Let's go to Montgomery Bell, and we'll go fishing." Tom didn't do much fishing; he spent most of his time in the water catching frogs and turtles. A picnic lunch would follow, sometimes with his brothers tagging along, but more often just Tom and his mother.

Tom was small for his age, and in elementary school, he was frequently picked on and pushed around. Finally realizing that it was better to get into a fight and deal with the aftermath than be pushed around, he got a reputation as a fighter. He wouldn't start it, but he was also done with being pushed around.

It wasn't always calm and peaceful at home, either. Tom was around thirteen and sitting at the dinner table after church. Roast beef was being served, as it often was, but Tom wanted something else. He asked, "Can't we have something else besides roast on Sunday?" His grandfather replied, "Bubba, if you don't like it, you can get up from the table," and Tom said, "Well, I don't like it." He walked up to his bedroom, which he shared with his brothers, went in, and slammed the door shut. Of course, that slamming door rang throughout the house on Spain Avenue. Almost before the sound had echoed away, the door came open again, hitting on the inside. Tom's grandfather busted him in the jaw and knocked him down. Right or wrong, Tom learned a lesson that day. Be appreciative of what you have.

Tom didn't hold that sore jaw against his grandfather. He loved him, and he knew that his grandfather loved him back. Tom understood anger. It would boil up inside of him, too, just like his grandfather. Just as quickly, it would go away. But first, he would run away, staying gone long enough for everyone in the family to get worried. When he would come back home, they would tell him they were going to send him to the bad boy school. The bad boy school – Jordonia, located in what is now Bordeaux, Tennessee – was a deterrent for young boys of that time. Considered the reform school for white boys for sixty years, the school could kindle fear in the hearts of misbehaving boys. Pikeville, Tennessee, housed the same type of reform school for the black boys. Both schools are now closed.

There seemed to be a family gene that was passed down from the grandfather, at least for the two older brothers. John was the baby, protected and taken care of often by the older boys. They all fought each other, as brothers do. While Howard was pretty laid-back and slow to anger, Tom remembers a time when he had been pushed too far.

Tom and his grandmother were in the front yard; he was watching her build a snowman. There was a contest in the neighborhood for the best snowman every year, and his grandmother had won first place for many years in a row. Howard and a friend were also outside, and Howard's friend threw a snowball at a car as it went by. The guy in the car stopped and got out. He mistakenly assumed that Tom's brother, Howard, had thrown the snowball. Tom told his grandmother to stop working on the snowman and watch; there was going to be a fight.

The guy walked up to Howard, bristling and ready to swing, and Howard hit him. Both of the guy's legs gave out, and the guy went down. He struggled to get back up, and Tom's grandmother yelled, "Boy, you better get back in that car." He did. Howard didn't need to hit him more than once. He was big and strong, a member of the track team, and a shot putter. Tom remembers that day well.

"My older brother was very low-key, but if he was pushed and it got to his limit, he would rise to the occasion. There is only one person in this world that I knew could whip me, just pick me up and whip me. That would be my older brother."

Tom grew up in the Methodist Church. His mother and grandmother were active in the Sunday school programs at Inglewood Methodist Church, and Tom was confirmed there. Confirmation for boys and girls would include a class that taught you about the Methodist Church and about what the Bible teaches.

Church was important during those years, those generations before Sundays became another weekend day. The 'Blue Laws' or 'Sunday Closing laws' were in effect in the 1950s and early 1960s, which prohibited retail and commercial sales on Sunday. No alcohol was legally sold on Sundays during the period. Family activities were held on Sunday afternoons, under the shade tree in the backyard.

Many families attended church on Sunday morning, Sunday night, and Wednesday night. Tom and his friends liked to sit in the balcony section, away from parent eyes and reproach. One Sunday, Tom was sitting next to his cousin, who bet him that he couldn't make a paper airplane and sail it down to the choir, which is at the front of the church. Tom, taking the bet, made the airplane and threw it with a gentle shove over the balcony rail. Floating up and down, looking like it was going to fall, then up again, finally landing right in front of the choir loft. Ruth Halliburton turned around in her seat and looked up. She knew where it came from and who had thrown it. She tried to be mad at her second son. But Tom wasn't in that much trouble. The choir wasn't all that exciting, and the little paper airplane had added a little something to the service that morning, enough so that the incident was talked about at the dinner table many times.

Tom's childhood seemed to be a time of proving something–proving that he was not going to be pushed around, that he would not be taken for granted. His temper was well-known to his teachers and friends. And God was knocking. Perhaps he didn't realize it at the time, or maybe he did. He has a distinct memory of sitting in church one morning listening to a visiting speaker. Dr. Rice was a missionary from South America. He shared his story, and something in Tom's heart spoke to him. He knew then that he might not be a missionary, but God had a plan for him, and it would be something like that. He didn't know where or when, but the seed had been planted.

Tom played ball with the neighborhood kids, but spent most of his time around a creek that ran close to his home, catching crawfish, salamanders, and snakes. His rebellion intensified during his middle school years.

Mr. Hooper was Tom's seventh and eighth-grade teacher; he had a paddle named the 'Meat Cleaver' and used it often on Tom's backside. Ruth was called whenever Tom would get a paddling, and she wasn't surprised. Her other sons were seldom in trouble, but she expected it of Tom. The other students weren't surprised either, remarking to one another,

'Halliburton is getting it again' when they heard the voice of Mr. Hooper say, 'Bend over and grab them.'

Tom was an academically strong student, a member of the Honor Society during his junior and senior years in high school. While he had walked to elementary school, hitchhiking was the preferred means of getting there during his high school years. Howard, his older brother, also hitchhiked, but didn't want Tom standing next to him, so Tom would stand a little behind until a car stopped. They would often have the same person stop each morning to give them a ride for the four miles to Isaac Litton High School.

"We didn't worry about bad people picking us up. We knew most of them. There was this one guy who was just evil and slimy. We called him Chicken Hawk. When Howard and I would see his car coming, we would hide."

Isaac Litton High School was built in 1930 and officially opened on October 25, 1930. While specific dates are not noted, the Halliburtons and Adwells (Tom's mother) graduated from Isaac Litton, as did many other relatives and friends of Tom and his family.

Tom had many friends attending Isaac Litton, as well as other schools that were nearby. *"On Friday and Saturday nights, we would get together and go to the*

Doghouse in Old Hickory for the music and dances. We all got to be good friends."

Author's Note:
As it has been called since the 1940s, the Doghouse still stands on Old Hickory Boulevard in Old Hickory. Once the high school gymnasium, it was also the site for sock hops and dances after football and basketball games. DuPont High School burned in November 1967, but the gym remained untouched.

Tom ran track in high school, winning races at the regional level. Shin splints prevented him from running at the state level, but his abilities had already given him a track scholarship to Middle Tennessee State College (now MTSU). Running cross-country races for the college during his first semester, Tom hitchhiked from his home in Nashville to Murfreesboro. Living in Smith Hall on campus, Tom met many boys who were also local, coming from Hendersonville, Madison, Maplewood, and DuPont high schools.

Tom had dated a lot in high school, and many of the girls were from surrounding areas and went to different schools. Tom graduated in 1964 and left high school for college, but not before falling in love with a girl from DuPont High School. Graduating in 1965, Pam left high school to attend college at Tennessee Tech University in Cookeville.

"I fell in love with her and thought she was in love with me. We had dated steady until she went off to Tech. A girl who knew Pam came up to me at the mailboxes at Middle. She told me that Pam wanted her to tell me that she wouldn't be able to commute and see me, and that the best thing to do would be to break up. She had told this girl that she knew I would understand.

I didn't. I was kind of numb; I remember that. I hitchhiked home to Nashville and got the drunkest I had ever been in my life."

Thankfully, Tom had friends who took care of him, driving him home and helping him get out of the car. But his troubles didn't end there. Tom was drunk and hurt and angry, loud and obnoxious. Howard, his brother, came out of the house and hit him, knocking Tom down. But that didn't stop Tom. His grandfather came out next and put him on the ground again. Tom's mother and grandmother put a stop to the fighting and took Tom inside; he was crying about what Pam had done to him. Aware that Tom had been drinking heavily, his mother was concerned about alcohol poisoning. She had heard about it and stayed up all night watching Tom, making sure he was okay.

Determined to put his heartbreak behind him and move on with his life, Tom returned to school. His determination soon faltered, and he began getting into trouble, fighting and drinking. Drinking in the dorm put him on social probation, and when he moved off campus the following year, the opportunities to get into more trouble surfaced.

Spending a night in the Gallatin (TN) Jail for being drunk and fighting didn't stop him from being in another fight in Smyrna (TN) and being arrested. The Judge in Murfreesboro was very blunt. He admonished Tom, telling him he would end up in jail, and suggested the military.

Tom was a young man, unfocused and adrift, and he knew he needed to do something different. His grade point average was low; he was going to flunk out. The very real possibility of being drafted was uppermost in his mind. The 1960s saw a rise in the military draft, primarily because of the Vietnam War. Between 1964 and 1973, over two million men were drafted, and the day was approaching when Tom knew he would be on the list. As the number of draftees increased in the mid-60s, many draft-eligible young men looked to recruiters to help them decide which branch they wanted to serve with before they were drafted into the Army.

Tom and a friend decided that they wanted either the Air Force or the Marines, so they split up and each one talked to a recruiter with the idea that they would compare notes and decide which one they would sign up with. If they didn't like either one, they would opt for the Navy. Their plans didn't pan out.

Tom talked to the recruiter with the Air Force, and he thought it would be the best military branch. He joined at the initial meeting. His friend did the same with the Marines. They didn't end up serving together, but they were okay with their choices. The time of service during the Vietnam War years was typically two years when you were deployed.

There was a quick turnaround when you joined up during the war years. Tom joined the Air Force on Monday. On Friday, he was given a physical and sworn in. Spending Friday night at a hotel reserved for the recruits, he called his mother and told her that he was leaving the next day on a bus for basic training. She was able to see him before he left for San Antonio. Seeing your son leaving for the military, especially during war, is a traumatic event. The worst that can happen must have occupied her thoughts, and she must have been on her knees many times in prayer.

Tom did basic training, just like everything else, bucking the system and causing problems. The training schedule called for eight weeks, but Tom had to do it twice, so it was sixteen weeks for him. An argument with his drill instructor led to shoving, and when Tom shoved him down the stairs, there were consequences. Keeping Tom in the office during his second attempt at basic training, his superiors were able to keep him contained and prevent him from fighting.

Tom spent a year at Whiteman Air Force Base in Knob Noster, Missouri. A strategic air command base in the sixties, the big bombers were housed there, and everyone could hear them going over the base. Classified in an administrative position, Tom was assigned to personnel, working in an office. He remembers a good roommate there, Rusty Conner[1]. "*He was a good friend, a hippie, a dope-smoking hippie from Ocean City, Maryland. He could really play a guitar. A really great guy.*"

Tom was ready for a change, and he found an opportunity through another serviceman. Bases in London and Vietnam were looking for volunteers. Tom

---

[1] Name changed.

volunteered to go to either one. London caught him first, and Tom spent over two years there, stationed at a Royal Air Force base, South Ruislip.

The US Air Force leased the station as an administrative base for US forces in the UK. It also housed the 7520th US Air Force Hospital and a school for children of American service personnel. It was here that Tom began his studies at the University of Maryland, and also where he met Lois' mother, who introduced him to Lois.

There were some minor scuffles in London, but thankfully, Tom handled them well. Good superiors helped; they liked Tom, and he appreciated them. Working in the publications distribution office, processing manuals and forms, Tom was not in situations that would lead to disagreements with other servicemen. He and his friends would 'let off steam' when they would go into Soho in London for entertainment.

"God had his hand on me. I can look back at that and see. I didn't go to church in London. There weren't a lot of services of anything like that around there. But something was going on."

Tom was honorably discharged from the Air Force in 1969. He and Lois were married and moved to Maryland, and Tom began working for the Montgomery County Police Department, where he was soon placed undercover.

CHAPTER SEVEN
(1980s)

Home Again & Cumberland City

Tom had looked at all the possibilities for seminary study. Emory in Georgia, Asbury in Kentucky, and Vanderbilt in Tennessee. With Tom's newfound spirituality, Asbury was a better fit, but he chose Vanderbilt and didn't apply anywhere else. Thinking he would be rejected since only a small percentage of applicants get in, Tom was, once again, testing his idea of being a full-time pastor. When God opened the door, Tom had to believe that God wanted him in the pulpit, finally. He wanted Tom to share his testimony in a different way than he had before, and there was no turning back.

The move was quick; thankfully, there was little to pack. Tom's mother had moved to McGavock Pike, and his grandmother had died, leaving his grandfather living alone in the house on Spain Avenue. Gayle began almost immediately working at the Methodist Publishing House, and Tom started his classes.

Vanderbilt is a non-denominational seminary, but at that time, more Methodists were going there than any other denomination. Many professors there had a strong John Wesley foundation and taught the history of the church from that viewpoint. Seminary professors, according to Tom, are mostly brilliant people, but spend most of their time in the 'ivory tower' studying and would find it challenging to lead a church as a pastor.

Seminary is academically challenging for many, but Tom had always been a good student when he pushed himself, and he fulfilled his promise to God. Tom stood true to the Biblical truths he had been taught since he was a child, and remained steadfast in his love for the Word of God.

"A lot of people, when they go to seminary, are swayed by the classes, by what is taught. They may go in believing the Bible, but they don't hang onto it. A strong foundation doesn't necessarily mean you can't be swayed. My foundation was not going to move, but some did. I had a very good friend there, Phillip. He started there as a very

liberal person; it was a second career for him, too, like me. As he listened in class and realized how ridiculous some of it was, he became ultra-conservative. A brilliant guy. It's unusual for that to happen, though. Most of the people coming out of there have been swayed; they are liberal and don't look at the Bible in the same way. They don't understand that you can't take scripture and make it say what you want it to. You have to look at the full context, what came before and what comes after."

Tom and Gayle had been living in Tom's grandfather's house for about three months when he received a phone call from a pastor at McKendree Methodist church. He wanted to meet with Tom and discuss an inner-city ministry that he was starting. He knew that Tom was in seminary and told him that he would like for Tom to head up the new ministry and thought it would be a good fit for him, since he would still be in Nashville.

Tom turned him down. He knew what he wanted, and he was reasonably sure that it was what God wanted him to do. He wanted a small church, a small community, something entirely different than what he had been accustomed to in his adult life. A student in seminary, working toward ordination, can pastor a church as a 'local pastor.' Tom approached Bob Spain, the District Superintendent (DS) of the Nashville district, and explained to him what he had in mind. If there were a place close enough to commute to classes at Vanderbilt, and a church that would accept a local pastor, Tom told the DS that he would like the opportunity. Bob Spain replied that he would talk to the other district superintendents and see what was available.

Cumberland City Methodist Church needed a pastor, and they were happy to have one who was also attending Vanderbilt to be ordained. Reverend Hunt was the Clarksville DS, and he approached Tom at Vanderbilt to discuss Tom's first appointment as a pastor. Cumberland City had a parsonage, so Tom would be commuting to Nashville for classes, which ended up being 170 miles round-trip each time he came to Vanderbilt. The appointment also included four other churches: Spring Hill Methodist, Cedar Valley Methodist, Lockert's Chapel, and Paul's Chapel. Tom would have at least two churches each Sunday, and often have three.

Loading up the station wagon once again with all of their belongings, Tom and Gayle, along with four children and a dog, make the trip to Cumberland City. It was a memorable trip. Gayle became car sick with the winding roads that went up and down and around hairpin curves. Crying, she complained about the drive and having to move so far away. It didn't take very long for Gayle to love their new home and all of the people that came with the change. But the beginning was a bit uncomfortable.

As Tom pulled into the driveway of their new home, the man who was meeting them came out the front door, talking very matter-of-factly after introductions. "I'm going to tell you right now. There's two things we don't want to hear about here. Number one, we don't want to hear any sermons about Shadrach, Meshack, and Abendego. And we don't want to hear sermons about the blood. It scares the kids."

Gayle managed to keep from laughing, but she also figured that they didn't need to unpack because she was pretty sure they wouldn't be staying there. The very first Sunday, she was certain that Tom would preach on precisely what he had been told not to talk about. She knew Tom well by that time.

Tom doesn't remember what he preached about the very first Sunday, but he was thankful to be there and remained there for over five years. Five years for five churches. Each one with a different size congregation, different needs, but all fond of Tom and his family. The members from all the churches got along well together, and all five would get together occasionally for special events. There were all kinds of people, from farmers to bankers and everybody in between.

One young man in Cumberland City was a frequent visitor to Tom's home there. Unfortunately, it was usually late on a Saturday night, and he would pull up in the driveway in an old truck and proceed to curse and scream at the house. Coming from what was considered a 'rough' family, the young man had a drug problem and remained a regular visitor to Tom's driveway on Saturday night for many months.

Cumberland City Methodist had a revival one spring; many members of the other churches under Tom's charge came to the revival. A member of the Cumberland City congregation ran a local grocery store and was well-known by everyone there. He had found out that he had throat cancer, and after the sermon, when Tom asked if there was anyone who wanted to speak one night at the revival, the man with cancer stood. "I can't really talk anymore, but I'm going to stand up right here until somebody gets saved tonight," he said. And he did stand there, but it didn't take very long for someone to come forward, asking to be saved. It was the young man who visited Tom's driveway on Saturday nights.

The following Saturday, the young man pulled into Tom's driveway again. But this time, although he was still yelling, he was screaming Hallelujah, over and over again. Jason, Tom's son, said, "Daddy, he's not cussing anymore!"

After the move from Nashville, Gayle had taken a position as an aide at the elementary school nearby, and Tom was preparing sermons for several churches and attending seminary classes in Nashville. Julie and the boys were in school. There were plenty of responsibilities to go around; it would be difficult to fit anything else in. But Tom managed.

Tom was busy with a service at the local cemetery, and two gentlemen came there to talk to him after he completed his talk. The school superintendent of Stuart County and one of the bank managers at Cumberland City Bank had a request. They needed an elementary school basketball coach, and they knew that Tom had played basketball. No other requirements were necessary.

"I loved basketball, and back then, I would say I probably knew as much as anybody else about coaching it around there."

The boys called Tom 'Brother Coach.' Sixth, seventh, and eighth-grade boys can be a handful, and on the basketball court, they would often display incorrect technique or forget the plays. Tom would stand on the sidelines, correcting their mistakes and offering advice. It was against the rules to stand on the sidelines, and the referee repeatedly told Tom to sit down. Finally, he said that he would have to call a technical on him if he did it again. So, Tom, instead of standing on the sideline, got down on one knee. He wasn't on the bench, but he wasn't standing up either. The referee didn't care and called a technical on him.

Tom knew the referee well, and he said, *"George, you know that I'm a preacher."*

George, the referee, nodded, and Tom said, *"Well, I'm praying."*

The referee began laughing and couldn't stop. Everyone could see him laughing.

Gayle was sitting in the stands. As Tom said, she was usually as quiet as a church mouse during these games, but this time she took a stand herself. "Ref, you can give him a technical, but you don't have to laugh at him!"

Tom loved his time with his first charges as a pastor. *"I was very blessed to be there. I learned a lot, more than anywhere I've ever been."*

Learning how to pastor, to reach the people who came to hear the Word, Tom considered it an honor and a blessing. Becoming not only a pastor, but a friend to those who looked to him for guidance, Tom speaks fondly of Fred Lyle, a member of the Spring Hill congregation. Fred ran the ambulance service for Houston County and would often receive a call on Saturday night, requiring him to be out most of the night before church on Sunday morning. Exhausted and sleepy, Fred would be in the pew. Fred had only just begun coming to church and wanted to continue to do so. He would start weaving; his eyes would close, and those around him would poke and punch at him to try to keep him awake.

Tom had noticed this repeatedly for a few weeks and decided that Fred needed help. Pulling him aside one Sunday after church, he offered advice. *"Fred, I know you're tired after working all night. Buy you some sunglasses. And when I start to preach, you put those sunglasses on."* Fred was surprised and questioned Tom. Wouldn't he care if one of the people in his church had on sunglasses? Tom assured him that he would not, and the following Sunday, Fred had on his new sunglasses. After the service was over, Fred came up to Tom and told him how much he appreciated his advice.

The story about the sunglasses would come back to haunt Tom down the road, however.

It was time for a change. The Methodist Conference doesn't usually allow a pastor to remain at one place for many years, and Tom was told that he would be moved to New Johnsonville. He had been serving the five churches for almost six years; he had finished his studies at Vanderbilt and had been ordained. It was time.

Moving again, and Gayle is crying. "I can't believe you're taking me away from my home in Cumberland City!" Almost every move would be tearful, leaving friends behind each time. The life of a pastor's wife is filled with emotional upheaval, especially in the Methodist Church.

Cumberland City UMC

"When I was attending Vanderbilt Seminary, there was this one girl in one of my classes. She came up to me while I was talking with someone else. I wasn't even talking to her. She walked up and said, 'I'm getting so sick and tired of you referring to God as He. You have offended God. Don't you think that it's offensive to God for you to limit Him to being a He?'

I told her that she was taking it up with the wrong person, and she said, 'What do you mean?'

I said, Well, we'll ask Jesus. He's the one who called him Father. Jesus referred to God the Father, and now, 2000 years later you come along and you've decided that you know more than Jesus did.

She answered, 'That's why nobody likes you here.' I replied, 'Does that mean I can't be involved in your wine tastings and all the social activities that I don't give a hoot about?'

Of course, that was the end of that conversation. That's who I am. I'm going to poke at people, make them think about what the truth is."

-Tom

88

CHAPTER EIGHT
New Johnsonville

New Johnsonville is about as far west as you can get in Middle Tennessee, right on the Tennessee River. Crossing the bridge, or the 'catfish curtain,' you would be in Camden or Humboldt, officially West Tennessee. New Johnsonville United Methodist Church had a beautiful parsonage in a nice neighborhood. A relatively new church, the membership included managers of the nearby Fossil Plant operated by the Tennessee Valley Authority. New Johnsonville UMC had another church attached to Tom's charge, Piska United Methodist Church. Piska's members were primarily the factory workers and farmers.

Humphreys County boasted excellent schools, and New Johnsonville's schools were no exception. Julie was attending Austin Peay University and working at a grocery store in Clarksville. Jason was entering high school; David was in middle school, and Mitchell was in the third grade. There was a wildlife refuge backing up to their large backyard, with woods for exploring and a small pond for fishing.

The churches grew under Tom's watch, and that was good for everyone, spiritually and financially. When Tom had first been told about his new appointment and had driven to New Johnsonville to look at the parsonage, the church treasurer met him at the house. Telling Tom that he didn't know how they were going to be able to pay his salary, Tom told him that he was sure they would figure it out and that he would be praying about it. Tom, thankfully, did get a raise. A preacher's salary, with four children, doesn't go very far.

Tom and Gayle were involved in their community in New Johnsonville, just as they had been in Cumberland City. The connections made in each appointment were permanent ones, lifelong friends. They attended school activities and school board meetings. One such meeting championed the esteem that the community held for Tom and Gayle. The problem being addressed concerned the closing of the local school, Lakeview Elementary. There was a plan in place to close the school and send the children to

Waverly. It would be a twenty- to thirty-minute bus ride to a different school. Several people were attending the meeting, and the New Johnsonville representatives asked Tom to talk to the school board and deliver a brief presentation outlining their concerns. Tom had no time to prepare, but he agreed.

The passionate speech he made about their desire to save their school, their love for their teachers, and how the teachers knew all the kids was important to the parents of the community. Tom told the board that although no one had anything against the school in Waverly, they were sure that it was a good school, too, but they wanted to keep their school.

The head of the school board was in attendance and took the podium next. Smiling, he told everyone that he was going to go out on a limb, and representing the board, said that they "accepted Brother Halliburton's proposal" and would continue to operate the school in New Johnsonville, Lakeview Elementary. 'Brother Halliburton' was well-known in the community, and not only to the Methodists that lived there.

After serving five churches in his first appointment and the two churches in his second appointment, Tom and Gayle formed many meaningful relationships. Friends that would show up in good times and, more importantly, in the hard times. Jimmy Lewis, Tom's named best friend, said, "Tom Halliburton has had his feet under every kitchen table in Houston, Stewart, and Montgomery County."

Tom did what he was called to do. He told his congregants about the love of Jesus, how God was there for each of them. He laughed with them, he cried with them. Tom loved people.

"Gayle talked me into this; she worked in a salon and she gave me a perm. We matched."

CHAPTER NINE
Livingston

Tom had been in the ministry for ten years when the Methodist conference moved him to Livingston. His appointments with the previous churches had been an ongoing spiritual adventure, leading him onward to a future in ministry that would bring joy and pain, faith and loss, and above all, a closer walk with Jesus. Tom and Gayle were fortunate that they were able to remain in Livingston for over thirteen years, most of it spent with Tom pastoring the Livingston United Methodist Church.

The first few weeks at Livingston were difficult but not without blessings. It is almost always hard to leave a church once you have made friends and relationships built on a mutual foundation of love for Jesus. Leaving New Johnsonville was no different. People on the church committee at New Johnsonville called Tom, begging him to come back. Tom explained to them why that couldn't happen, but he did counsel with them. They had been given a pastor who was involved in an extramarital affair, and they were concerned with the direction he would take the church. Tom talked with them several times over the first few months of the pastoral change, and eventually, New Johnsonville was once again a happy church.

Tom and Gayle had heard a lot about Livingston. One of the district superintendents told Tom that it was a beautiful place; there was camping at Standing Stone State Park, a YMCA camp, and Dale Hollow for fishing and scuba diving. It wasn't uncommon for the incoming pastor to visit the parsonage, so Tom and Gayle drove to Livingston to see what they would need when they moved.

The parsonage, although a nice home, was filthy and hadn't yet been cleaned. The chairperson of the Staff/Parish committee was there with them, as well as the outgoing pastor. Gayle mentioned to the chairperson that she and Tom had a dog, and the outgoing pastor spoke up, saying, "I wouldn't let anyone move into a parsonage with an animal," and the chairperson turned to him and said, "I'll tell you this. My dog is cleaner than that bowl that's in your dishwasher and your sink right now. And cleaner than this whole house is." Tom and Gayle kept their dog.

"I didn't like Livingston at first, but I came to love it. It was a change, that's all. It was harder to get to know people there than it had been in Cumberland City and New Johnsonville. I could go to a restaurant anywhere close to New Johnsonville and Cumberland City, and everybody knew me, and I knew them. At Livingston, I didn't know anyone, and it seemed like they didn't want to know me. It's different everywhere you go, so I guess this was my first time with such a different beginning."

By the time Tom had been moved to Livingston, their daughter, Julie, had graduated from Austin Peay and married. Five years older than Jason, she was teaching school, and her first child, Rhett, was born the summer that Tom and Gayle moved to Livingston. Jason would begin his senior year in high school at Livingston Academy, a public high school. David was beginning his second year of high school. Mitchell was living in Florida with his mother and attending school there.

Almost immediately upon Tom's arrival in Livingston, two of the older ladies of the congregation asked to meet with him. They expressed a complaint about his predecessor, and they were hopeful that Tom would correct that problem. His predecessor never visited anyone, and the ladies had prepared a list of names of those people who no longer attended church. They wanted Tom to see them. Tom expressed his doubts about the outcome of those visits but agreed to do so, and asked that the ladies accompany him to the homes of the people on the lists. They agreed, and, after a few visits, understood. The reasons why the people didn't return were still unknown, but the purpose of the visits failed. Tom's experience had shown him that when people stopped coming to a church, something had happened that is usually never revealed to the pastor. Hopefully, they find another church family that speaks to their heart and allows them to follow Jesus and not simply use the church as preparation for their funeral.

Visiting new attendees and members of the church was not a new thing for Tom; he had visited many during his ten years of ministry. But Livingston was different. When Tom first arrived in New Johnsonville, one of the first things he was told was that they didn't expect him to come and visit them. "We know where your house is; we can find you," they had told him.

One place many believers do want to see their pastor, besides in the pulpit, is when they are in need and hurting. That is often in the hospital. While not expected, Tom made many rounds of hospitals while serving a congregation. During his time in Livingston, he may have driven from St. Thomas or Vanderbilt Hospital in Nashville, Tennessee, to Erlanger Hospital in Chattanooga, and then on to Knoxville for Fort Sanders Hospital, all in the same day. There were also local hospitals, Livingston Hospital and Cookeville Hospital.

Tom was also pastoring Shiloh Methodist, a smaller church, with his appointment at Livingston. Traveling there each Sunday before his sermon at Livingston, he didn't realize he wasn't expected to be there every week. Shiloh had been assigned a part-time pastor. Tom was surprised to learn from one of the members of Shiloh that the congregation appreciated his dedication to their little congregation and enjoyed his sermons, even though their previous pastor was only there occasionally. However, Tom felt led to continue serving the congregation each week and did so.

The first year at any new church has changes for both the pastor and his family and the congregation. Some of the changes had little to do with the church, but were simply part of moving to another town. Tom and Gayle had two boys in school, and both were moving into a new town, with new faces and new challenges. David's coach at his previous school in Waverly wanted to find a way for David to stay with someone else and continue to play basketball for Waverly. An outstanding player, Waverly tried to keep him, but that was not to be. David remained with his parents and played basketball for Livingston.

Jason's senior year also had challenges for both Jason and his parents.

"One night, I got a phone call from the sheriff there in Livingston. He says, 'I don't know what kind of son you're raising, Reverend Halliburton, but the other night he and a bunch of other boys were in his pickup truck and he backed out and backed over and destroyed part of one of my fences. What are you going to do about it?' I asked him, 'What do you want me to do about it?"

The sheriff told Tom that he should send Jason up to the sheriff's farm, and he would "work his a** off on Saturday." Tom replied that he would send Jason up there. Jason goes and never argues about it. He comes back home, and the following week he goes again. He doesn't say anything about it and continues to go for two more weekends. Tom asks Jason to have the sheriff call him. The sheriff calls Tom the next Saturday.

"I don't know what kind of parent you are, making that boy come up here. One of the finest young men I've ever met. You ought to be ashamed of yourself." Tom was flabbergasted. He asked Jason what they had been doing on all these Saturdays. Jason said that he would work for two or three hours, and then he and the sheriff would sit on the bed of his truck and talk.

The time is close for Jason to finish high school, and he says that he might not graduate. Jason was a mediocre student and likely didn't pay as much attention to his studies as he could have. Very popular with students and adults alike, he got along with everyone and was active in the church that Tom was assigned to. Jason told Tom and Gayle that it would be okay, because everyone would be getting a tube when they walked up in front of everyone at graduation. He was pretty sure that his would be empty, however, and not have a diploma in it.

Graduation night arrived, and Jason walked up to the school superintendent and took the tube. As he stood in front of the camera, he decided to open up the tube and look inside. He pulls out his diploma, and yells out to everyone, "It's in there!" Tom and Gayle cried; everyone else laughed.

Jason went to Florida after graduation and got a job, living with his mother. "I promise you I'm coming back," he told Tom and Gayle, and they knew it was true. He had gone to see his mother and his little brother, Mitchell, who was in the eighth grade.

Jason started attending a Baptist church near his mother's home. He called Tom and told him that the pastor at the church said that Jason needed to be baptized. Tom told him that if that was the church he wanted to go to, he should probably go ahead and do it. But Jason was hesitant. He said that he had told the preacher that his father had baptized him. Tom understood his quandary.

"Okay, Jason, tell him that you were baptized in Wells Creek. I baptized you there so that the water flowed over you and away from you, right out into the Cumberland River, because I wasn't going to let your sins stay and hang around you. It took the sin away down into that river. Tell him that."

Jason called his father back and told him that he had repeated what Tom had told him. The Baptist preacher had said to him that he felt that was good enough, and he didn't see any point in doing it again. Jason had been in Florida about six months.

Another phone call from Florida would be the one that could have burned Tom's soul, destroying his faith. But Tom's God, the only true Jehovah, the One that Tom promised to follow, held him close.

CHAPTER TEN
Jason

"I got a call about four o'clock in the morning. It was March of 1993. They said 'Is this Tom Halliburton?' And I said, Yes, it is. My first thought was that the call was probably from the coach at Livingston Academy. David was playing basketball at the state tournament, and I thought that perhaps David wanted me to come and get him. I listened to the man on the other end of the line, and it was not David's coach. 'This is the Duval County Police Department.' They told me my son, Jason, had been murdered.

The church where Gayle and I were married, the one where I was the youth leader, had a large parking lot with basketball goals set up. Jason and some friends were playing ball in the lot. Two other sets of boys were having some problems that had grown into a confrontation. One *set of boys was gathered on one side of the parking lot, and the other group was walking down the street. Jason and his friends weren't in either group, but somehow one of the boys moved into Jason's group. Then the shots were fired. Missing the one he was shooting at, one of his bullets struck Jason in the back, and another boy in the leg. It was just a bunch of kids, mad because someone had their hat turned around the wrong way.*

The police arrived at the scene almost immediately, and believed that Jason likely died instantly. They arrested the young man who fired the gun.

Someone picked up David and brought him home. All of a sudden, our house was full of people; they were there for us. People from Livingston, people from New Johnsonville, people from Cumberland City. I didn't know what to do; we were at a loss. We had never had anything like that happen to us. I thought I was the kind of person who could handle anything, but I found out I was wrong. I was a basket case. I paced back and forth around the house. There was a man from church sitting in a chair. I would go by him, and each time he would ask if there was anything he could do. I said no. No, over and over again. What could anyone do?

We felt that the funeral would be easier to have in Florida for many reasons. We were on our way to Florida, and David was in the back seat. He had been so quiet, saying nothing for such a long time after he heard about his brother. David was crushed; he idolized Jason. We're approaching Monteagle Mountain, on the way up over the ridge, when David spoke up.

'Dad, we know where Jason is. He's in heaven. I know he is. But what do we do?'

I said, 'About what, David?'

He said, 'About the boy that killed him.'

And I said, after a short pause, 'David, we're Christians. We forgive.'

David didn't say anything for a long time."

Author's Note:
As Tom was telling me this, I sat in amazement. The pain of loss was evident in his tone and on his face. Yet there was no anger or hatred for the boy responsible for Jason's death. I'm sure there are many, like me, who would have reacted, out of grief, naturally, in a revengeful way. But not Tom. He knew where Jason was, and his faith, even though Satan had tested him to the brink of despair, was strong and took him through. Proof that God is with us in our grief. Tom and Gayle exhibited that faith when it seemed like their world was collapsing around them.

"The preacher that Jason had talked to about baptism did the funeral. We found out more about the kind of man Jason had become while we were there. It was the same there as in Livingston and New Johnsonville. Everybody knew him and loved him. Jason worked at a car dealership in Jacksonville, and his boss came to the funeral. He told us that we wouldn't be able to imagine how many people he witnessed to there at the dealership, and the impact he had on their lives. It wasn't exactly what I expected, to be honest. We never said that Jason was perfect; he wasn't, but we did find out the good soul he was.

We came back home after the funeral, and it had started snowing. It was March, but we got seventeen inches of snow up on the plateau. It was good; I wasn't ready to preach, and all the churches were closed. I had another week to prepare. I needed to think about what I was going to say. Finally, I knew what I needed to say. The first service after Jason died was short. I said, 'I know that a lot has happened, and here's the bottom line. We have forgiven that man. It doesn't mean that we agreed with anything, but we have forgiven him. He's a young man. He has his whole life to live, and hopefully it'll turn out well for him. We never got his name, and we're not looking for it.'

We're dealing with a lot. But God showed up every day. People from New Johnsonville came and sat with us. People from Cumberland City were there. And then more people *began coming to church; more and more people. The love of the Lord bore down on us. All these people loving on us and helping us to pray. We weren't angry at God; I know some people feel that way. We prayed a lot. We prayed for the Holy Spirit to minister to us. We prayed for our lives to be better, for us not to have to live the rest of our lives with this pain. I just felt like the devil had one victim, and he wasn't getting another.*

A short time later, there was a gathering of kids in the Tennessee Methodist conference at Beersheba. Gayle and I were there with David, and I asked a group of them to tell me any stories they had about Jason, anything they might remember about him. This one girl, she said, 'Brother Tom, when we were at Paris Landing, I remember Jason climbed up the elevator shaft.'

I remembered when that happened. When I came to pick up the church group of kids at Paris Landing, the pastor in charge told me that a kid had climbed up the elevator shaft and no one would tell on him. As I'm driving the church bus back, I'm yelling at the kids, asking them who did it. They never would tell me. I had no idea it was Jason. David never did tell on him, either, and he was there. Stories like that, well, it helps to remember and laugh about it."

"When we were in New Johnsonville, Jason was just a kid, a well-liked kid. He was a good kid, a normal boy. He was always outside playing ball or something. When he died, the people at New Johnsonville wanted to hold a service for him, and they had a plaque made to honor him."

                    -Tom

Question: When you get to Heaven, what is the first question you'll ask and who will you ask?

Tom: *"Jesus. I'll ask him, Where is Jason?"*

CHAPTER ELEVEN
Up on the Hill

The love that surrounded Tom, Gayle, and David continued to guide them to a peace they dared not hope for. God sent many people to them, praying with them, talking with them, and the church continued to grow.

"I had been like the father of the church, you know, and then, during the hardest time, they allowed me to be loved on, they loved on us. The church started growing because of that, all that love. I don't think people believe it when I tell them. Everybody knew Jason."

Tom, Gayle, and David were living in the parsonage. When the church committee asked if there was anything that they could do to help him, Tom requested a housing allowance, and he was able to purchase the parsonage. Next came a totally unexpected gift from the Cates brothers. The brothers were members of the Livingston church; one was a doctor and the other a realtor. They gave Tom and Gayle eight beautiful acres in Willow Grove and suggested that they build on the property. It was a stunning site for a home, and they approached another member of the church, Lewis Oakley. Mr. Oakley was a builder, and he became the contractor, refusing to accept any payment for his services. With Tom and Gayle covering the labor and materials costs, they were able to build a comfortable home with a beautiful view. David had graduated from high school by the time the house was built; he was working for Lewis and taking some classes at a satellite campus for Vol State University. David helped build his parents' home, and as a loving tribute to Jason, the Bible given to Jason at his confirmation, with his name inscribed in it, was placed in the cornerstone of the home. Jason and David's presence was felt in the home, and blessed, Tom and Gayle were able to live there for several years.

David had a tough time dealing with Jason's death and eventually signed up for the Air Force, surprising Gayle and Tom. He served his country for ten years, stationed in Kuwait, Afghanistan, and South Korea. He was a crew chief for the A-10 Warthog, responsible for all maintenance on the plane. Prayer and perseverance helped him tackle his PTSD issues, which he is able to, thankfully, control. David continued his education upon his honorable discharge from the Air Force, earning an MBA at the University of Phoenix extension in Nashville.

Tom and David had enjoyed a close relationship since David was small. At the adoption proceedings, when the Judge asked David if he wanted Tom to be his dad, David answered, "He IS my daddy."

Tom was concerned about David when he joined the Air Force; he had been very quiet and spoke very little. Julie assured Tom that he would be okay. "He's mad at the world. He knows he can be mad at you and you'll love him anyway." Tom knew David was still dealing with Jason's death, but wasn't sure how to approach him. When David said that he had three days off with pay before leaving, he asked to spend them with Tom and go fishing. Tom agreed and was sure that they could discuss things on the trip.

Praying, Tom asked God to lead him to say and do what David needed. Three days of fishing, talking about nothing in particular, and Tom felt he had failed. Returning home, Tom takes his dog for a walk and prays. *"Lord, I blew it."* But that still, perfect voice told Tom that he had not failed. So, he waited. David comes to him and says, "I love you, Dad," and Tom replied, "I *love you, too,*" and David went on to say, "Dad, I've got to tell you something. This has been the three best days of my life." God knew what David needed and led Tom to be quiet, letting the days unfold as they should. David just wanted them to be together. God knew it, and then Tom did, too.

Julie and David deeply felt the loss of Jason in their lives, and the faith that Tom and Gayle had instilled in them helped them in their grief and gave them the knowledge that they would see him again. Mitchell was in Florida at the time of Jason's death, and Tom and Gayle prayed for him as well. Since Mitchell had opted to live with his mother several years earlier, he had not been able to sustain a close relationship with his brother until Jason moved to Florida. Mitchell was in the seventh grade when Jason was killed.

It was very difficult for both Tom and Gayle when Mitchell decided he wanted to live in Florida. Both Jason and Mitchell had been with Tom and Gayle for several years, along with Julie and David. When one is missing, it becomes difficult to make adjustments. God calmed Tom's anxiety. "*I prayed every day about Mitchell when he decided to stay there after a visit. I was worried about him. I prayed and prayed. 'Please, God, don't let anything happen to Mitchell.*"

The Holy Spirit was moving in Livingston through Tom's testimony and the love that was evident in the people who walked into the church building. The church began to grow, with each Sunday bringing more people who wanted to hear about what was happening there.

Tom was invited to speak and give his testimony at other churches. One such church was in Smithville. Kathy, Livingston's youth leader also came, with a group of the youth, to Smithville to hear Tom. Kathy's husband ended up at the altar that night, requesting that the Holy Spirit come into his life; he told Tom that he wanted his family to have the relationship that Tom and Gayle enjoyed with the Holy Spirit.

Livingston UMC began to earn, rightfully so, a reputation. Depending on the denomination, the reputation that spread could be bad or good. Some even dropped to a level of calling Tom the Anti-Christ. They couldn't understand the glory of the Holy Spirit and what happened when someone allowed the Spirit to work in their lives.

The power of God was moving. The Livingston church grew; people were hearing that something was going on in Livingston, and they wanted to be a part of it. The youth group was praying at the flag at the school.

The youth director had everyone praying around the schools in the county. Spiritual warfare was marching around the schools, praying for everyone in the schools, and then praying at the county courthouse.

There was a small public housing section in Livingston. A poor county, many at the church would encounter those who were mentally and emotionally disturbed. One man would ride up and down the road in an electric wheelchair. He had lived in Nashville previously, where he had been burned in an altercation with other problematic people. Ending up in the public housing of Livingston, he had a rebel flag on his wheelchair and would ride around, cussing out everyone. Some of the youth at Livingston knew who he was and started praying for him, praying often and together. One Sunday morning, he comes to church. One of the girls with the youth group went to him and hugged him. This broken man made it to the altar and accepted the Lord.

Tom had always felt a spiritual leaning towards a healing ministry. It was no different in Livingston. Sunday nights would often include a healing service in the chapel. Always attended to capacity, Tom prayed about the services and felt God leading him to move the service to Sunday morning. The Holy Spirit assured him that people would come from the North, from the

South, from the East, and from the West to help in this new ministry. Tom responded by moving the services to Sunday morning, and the miracles happened. Both for those who were sick and in answer to God's call. A surgeon from one direction, a pediatrician from another, a family doctor from the opposite, and another physician for the remaining direction. All ended up at Livingston, looking for a home church. Physical ailments were addressed, prayed over, and numerous healings occurred.

Miracles continued to happen; people were healed, and the word spread. People came from the surrounding area to see what was happening there. Some came to prove it was impossible; some came who were curious and had questions. Many didn't believe what they saw with their own eyes.

A DS – district superintendent - came. Tom could tell that he wasn't comfortable with the proceedings, and Tom didn't have an opportunity to speak with him before he left. However, the DS called Tom on Monday morning and asked to see him. Tom agreed and made the trip to the DS office. The DS said, "Tommy, I want you to understand this. I'm not coming back to your service." When Tom asked him why not, the DS replied that he was totally uncomfortable, even though he did not doubt the healing and sincerity of what was taking place. When Tom replied that he had noticed his uneasiness, the DS said, very plainly, "Please don't stop doing it."

"I'm not sure what makes a preacher uncomfortable with people being healed. It has something to do with the Holy Spirit. We have head knowledge, some heart knowledge, but not full understanding. Many Christians become uncomfortable when such things happen. It's so dynamic, and some don't know how to participate in something so different."

Tom entered the church in Livingston during a time when many churches were experiencing a drop in attendance. The average attendance was approximately two hundred on Sunday morning and 90 for Sunday School. God was at work in Livingston, and He placed Tom there for a purpose. Small groups were formed, sometimes meeting at the church building, and some held in congregants' homes. The small groups grew in number, while Sunday school attendance remained the same, and attendance in church services increased threefold over the next few years. The youth group became strong and active.

The excitement in Livingston continued to grow. New experiences emerged, and outreach became a vital component in the church's growth. Belmont

Community Church had been conducting a mission trip in Mexico for several years and, looking to redirect their resources, called upon Livingston UMC to take over their mission in El Oro, Mexico. The church at Livingston was excited at the prospect of expanding its ministry. Tom and Gayle took a group to El Oro, where they found a different dynamic than is normal in the United States. At that time, in Mexico, you were generally either a Christian or a Catholic. There was a separation of the two, unable to keep the common ground as a link between them.

Tom and Gayle are with the 'Christian' designation, and the group is there to have a Vacation Bible School for the children and a revival with the storefront ministry in the city. The area was not particularly good, and there could be repercussions. A 'gringo' (Tom) is coming to preach, and the word gets out. There could be a problem. The head of a cartel that is primarily known for selling drugs has made it known that he is going to put a stop to this 'gringo' preaching. Aware of the possibility of violence, Tom refuses the local minister's offer to step down.

With Gayle on one side and the interpreter on the other, Tom stood at the front of the crowd of people gathered there to hear the gringo. Suddenly, an aisle opened up in the middle of the crowd, and a man ran down the opening, yelling in Spanish. As he neared the front of the church and before he reached the pulpit, Tom returned the yell with a firm tone. *"Devil, I repel you in Jesus' name. You are not going to hurt me. You are going to come to know Jesus."*

The cartel member stopped in his tracks and began crying, whimpering. The dangerous drug leader, now sobbing, went to Gayle. And she held him. He cried the rest of the service with Gayle holding him. Calming, the cartel leader came to know the Lord that night. Though Tom and Gayle never saw him again, he was in good hands with the local minister.

Another mission trip took several from the Methodist organizations in Tennessee to Lyon, Mexico. There was a Methodist mission in Lyon, but it was tough to reach by any vehicle. The men and women from Tennessee were there to help clear some land so that the mission could build a road. There was a small church nearby, and everyone decided to go. Tom didn't realize until they were on the way that he was expected to share his testimony; he hadn't had time to prepare, but he was honored to be asked. He met one of the pastors there before he stood to give his testimony. The pastor told him that they tried to keep the noise down; there was a Catholic church nearby, and they didn't want any disturbances. The same strange relationship between Christians and Catholics existed in Lyon, as it did in most of Mexico. The Christians, who were at this small church, were often mistreated by the Catholics. It was a peculiar situation that was difficult for any visitor to understand. It would be impossible to ascertain the specifics of the separation between the two involved without speaking to both, and that didn't happen while Tom was there.

The pastor told Tom that if the people in the church agreed with what he was saying, they would wave their bulletins. There would be no yelling out Hallelujah or Amen, only the waving of bulletins. Tom began to preach and gave his testimony. The waving started and continued throughout his talk. *"I've never experienced that much quietness during any sermon I've ever done."*

Returning to Livingston, Tom was appreciative of being in a country where sounds from the Christians were expected, and rejoiced.

The secretary at Livingston, Amy Fletcher, was a blessing to Tom and Gayle. Very young when she started working at the church, she remained there for many years. Tom came out of his office one morning and told her that he was going over to the hospital. He was having pretty intense chest pains, but didn't want anyone to know. Amy, of course, was concerned, but we don't know who she did call, even though Tom had told her not to.

Tom went to Livingston Hospital, but after the doctor checked him over, he was sent immediately to St. Thomas in Nashville. Since the medical helicopter was busy in Chattanooga, he would be going by ambulance. Gayle had to follow as best she could in her car.

"I tried telling the doctor there, Dr. Cates, that I didn't have any blockages. I was looking at the same screen he was. He said something like, 'Listen, Reverend. You're not my spiritual father. I'm the doctor. Don't tell me what you see on these screens. I'll tell you.'

There were lots of tests, and I did the treadmill test. Finally, they told me that I did have a blockage, but it had cleared up on its own. This doctor said, 'No, I know you, Tom, and I know that you're a Christian and you might call this a miracle, but it's not unusual for this to happen.' I told him, 'Well, I'll still call it a miracle.'

I wasn't afraid; I'm not scared of anything like that. I think if a doctor told me that I had six weeks to live, I wouldn't be frightened. I would be okay with having people pray over me, and of course, I would pray for healing. I would also pray for God to do His will. I'm a firm believer. I'm going to heaven."

Tom prayed over many sick and hurting people, some of whom were at church and some in the hospital. One in particular sparked a memory. A member of the Livingston church asked Tom to go and see her Uncle Bob[1] in the hospital, saying that her Uncle didn't know the Lord. Tom immediately agreed, but when he pulled into the hospital parking lot, he was concerned. He didn't really want to do it, even though he knew that God had led him there. Praying for someone who doesn't want or appreciate your concern is a weight to carry.

As Tom got out of his car, he noticed four of the 'church ladies' coming out of the hospital. There was a chance he wouldn't need to go in, but the idea was fleeting. One of the ladies saw Tom and told him that Bob wouldn't let them come in. The man was in intensive care, but wouldn't allow the church ladies in.

Tom went into the ICU and told the nurse that he wanted to see Bob. The nurse replied that Bob would not be happy about seeing a pastor, but Tom insisted.

As the nurse opened the curtain, Bob looked out and saw Tom. He asked, "I know who you are. What are you doing here?"

---

[1] Name changed.

Tom responded, *"I'm here to pray for you."*

Bob didn't want Tom there with him, but Tom didn't give him a choice. He shared his testimony, his life story with Bob. Bob was quiet during Tom's talk, and when Tom finished, Bob said, "I've got one thing to say."

Tom nodded, and Bob continued, "You're worse than I ever was. You're worse than I am right now."

Tom smiled down at Bob and took his hand.

"Yeah, that's right, I guess. And I'm saved now, and filled with the Holy Spirit. I'm asking in Jesus' name if you accept Him as your Lord and Savior."

Bob replied, "I believe I do."

Tom shook his head. *"No, I need for you to say whether you do or not, for sure,"* and Bob replied, "Yes, I do."

Bob lived another six months. He would point Tom out to his friends and tell them that Tom was the person he had been talking about. Bob came to church, and his niece was so happy. Bob was there for any church event. Before Bob passed away, he asked to see Tom. He was in the hospital, and he knew that his time was short.

"Tom, it's okay. I'm happy. I'm fine; I know where I'm going, you know. Problem is, I've got to ask you a favor. I really want to have my funeral at the church; I want you to do it. But none of my friends will come if it's in the church, so just have it at the funeral home, okay?"

"That's what we did. I've had things like that happen several times; someone doesn't want you to come in, they don't want you in the room where they're dying. It's not that unusual. Sad, but not unusual. As a preacher, you wonder how much good it does when you go in and see somebody and they don't want you to be there. With Bob, I didn't want to go. But I told God I would go where He sent me. And I was blessed."

CHAPTER TWELVE
Emmaus

Several groups from the church were traveling to Nashville to attend Emmaus weekends. The Emmaus weekend program is inspired by the Gospel of Luke (Luke 24:13-35): Two disciples are walking to the town of Emmaus. The Risen Christ joins them on their walk and speaks with them, discussing scripture, but they don't know who He is until He reveals Himself to them. This weekend retreat offers a disciplined study of Christianity as a way of life, including talks, worship, and Holy Communion. The weekend inspires leaders of church groups and helps Christians to realize this potential in living for Christ in their daily lives. Emphasizing God's grace, the program has helped renew missions worldwide.

There were so many from the Livingston area and surrounding areas who attended the Emmaus weekends in Nashville that the Cumberland district members decided there was a need for an Emmaus community in Livingston. Tom's church was the perfect place to host the weekend retreat; it had a family life center, a gym, and ample space for the meetings. The Emmaus weekends began, and more people came to know the Holy Spirit.

Livingston UMC

Shiloh UMC

Tom and Gayle, however, didn't know how very different the Emmaus weekends would be in Livingston. Several church ladies had returned from a retreat and urged Tom and Gayle to attend the Vineyard Church in Toronto to hear about the great things happening there. With the church ladies paying for the trip, Tom and Gayle finally agreed after refusing several times. The church, known as the Toronto Blessing, was enormous. Held in a converted factory, parts of the sanctuary were carpeted. Called 'carpet time,' the rug was where people would go at the end of the service for prayer.

Thousands of people were there for the service Tom and Gayle attended. They came from everywhere: Germany, Japan, many US states, and Canada. After the service, Tom and Gayle decided to go to the back, where the carpet prayer time was held. Jamie Buckingham's church was represented there, ready to pray for people. A master storyteller and Bible teacher, Jamie Buckingham had authored many well-received books in the Christian community and beyond. A young lady represented Buckingham's church, and they both began praying with Tom and Gayle. Gayle suddenly told Tom that she was very hot. Gayle said, 'This is not a hot flash,' and then she moved and fell onto the carpet. Tom and the young lady continued to pray over Gayle; she spoke about seeing God and touching the Lord. On the floor for several minutes, Tom knew that he was meant to be a witness to this beautiful event.

"Gayle rises, and then we go to the hotel room. We talk about it, we talk a lot, and then we go back, again and again, to the church. It's really hard to explain. It brought

us closer together, Gayle and I. It's hard to tell what happened; we were still young in the Spirit. We never questioned what was going on. We didn't understand it, but we were happy and excited. Excited to get back home and share it."

Returning to Livingston, Tom gets up to preach his Sunday sermon. After the service, Tom prays with one of the ladies, and she falls to the floor, filled with the Holy Spirit. As Tom continues to pray for her, he realizes that the Holy Spirit is there, just as the Spirit was in Toronto, strong and full of grace and love.

The Emmaus weekend was the following weekend; it was a men's retreat.

"I'm walking up to go into the sanctuary, and I feel God tell me to start singing 'Amazing Grace.' Now I can't think of anything that the Holy Spirit would ask me to do that would make me more uncomfortable than singing. It's not my thing at all, but when God tells me to do something, I do it. I'm singing as I'm walking in there."

God always has a plan. As Tom is walking in and singing, a large man comes out of one of the pews and picks Tom up. He puts Tom on the other side of the chamber rail at the front of the church. The man gets down on his knees and tells Tom, "I'm not getting up from here until I get saved."

Tom prays with him and tells him to lift his arms. Tom holds his hands under his arms and prays for Jesus to give the man what he needs, repeating it over and over. The arms go higher and higher until he crashed down on the altar rail. The Holy Spirit moved that night during the Emmaus service, as everyone there prayed and sang. A service that usually lasts a couple of hours continued until well after 4:00 a.m.

The same happens the following weekend at the women's Walk to Emmaus. The women's leader asked Tom to come and bless them. Gayle was able to be present when the Spirit moved among all the women, praying and holding women, crying and praising Jesus with them.

The Emmaus community has a national presence, and the lay leader asked to speak to Tom. He told Tom that some people were pretty upset about what was happening. With Tom now realizing that those who can't understand are frightened by something they haven't experienced themselves, he realizes their unease. Some people don't want to experience it, fearing what it would be like. The lay leader of the Emmaus national community wondered what the people there, who were from other denominations, thought about the experience. Tom told him that everyone was either on the floor or shouting and saying

'Hallelujah,' praising God. He couldn't tell one denomination from another.

God told Tom what to do. And Tom promised God that he would follow Him. What joy that he did.

> *"Remember the thing with the sunglasses back at Spring Hill Methodist? Fred wearing his sunglasses because he was so tired? One night at Livingston, we were having a Bible study, and I told them about what happened with Freddie and the sunglasses. My Sunday morning services were live on the local radio station. So, I get up, ready to preach the next Sunday morning and suddenly, around three hundred people in the congregation put on sunglasses. I started laughing, and they all started laughing. Of course, the people listening on the radio didn't know what was going on."*
>
> *–Tom*

CHAPTER THIRTEEN
Cookeville
District Superintendent

There was significant spiritual growth at Livingston during Tom's tenure there. Things were changing in the Methodist Church, and pastors were allowed to remain at their charges for more extended periods. Tom and Gayle were at Livingston United Methodist for eleven years, and witnessed the numbers rise to six hundred attending on Sunday morning. Tom had brought the Emmaus program to Livingston; the church had ample space and provisions to provide for the weekend events that would lead to many leaders in the Christian faith.

There were signals that Tom would remain at Livingston for the remainder of his ministry. Tom had made an enemy of sorts with the appointed Bishop of the area. At a district meeting, Tom had interrupted the Bishop's speech, calling him out on what he was talking about. The Bishop was admonishing all of the pastors at the meeting, telling them that they needed to be ministering to the poor; he believed that they were neglectful in seeing the value of such a ministry.

Tom and many of the pastors present were heavily involved in their ministries to the poor and everyone they came into contact with. Tom, not one to mince words, spoke up.

"Bishop, I think I saw you just pull up in a big Buick, and I know where you live. You live in a gated community. And I know where most of us live, and it ain't no gated community. Give it all up, and I'll follow you anywhere you want me to go. But until you give it up, don't stand there and lecture me about something you don't know about me. Whether I'm innocent, poor, or not, and you use me as an example? I've got a pickup truck out there."

Tom was happy at Livingston, but his calling out the Bishop didn't help his relationship with the cabinet. There were other issues at play. The Board at Livingston United Methodist had considered leaving the Methodist Church. There were changes that many disagreed with and felt were neither biblical nor appropriate. The Board decided, with Tom trying to keep his distance from the proceedings, to ask the Bishop to answer seven questions, either in person or by letter. Tom remembers five of the seven questions:

1. Does our church believe in the virgin birth?
2. Does our church believe in the physical resurrection of Jesus Christ?
3. Does our church believe that scripture is the true word of God?
4. Does our church believe that homosexuality is a sin?
5. Does our church believe that marriage is between one woman and one man?

The Bishop opted to come to Livingston and answer the questions in person, and at that time – this was in the 1990s – he answered all of the questions 'yes.' But he also had a message for Tom.

"Tom, you'd better hope you never leave here because there's not an appointment for you anywhere else in Tennessee."

Tom told him that it was okay. He was happy in Livingston and didn't care if he ever left there. But it was not to be.

Bishops change, and a close friend and mentor, Bill Morris, became the next Bishop. Bishop Morris approached Tom at a mutual meeting and told him that he had been hearing some things about him. Some things that didn't surprise him at all, but also good things.

Tom told Gayle that he had an idea that Bishop Morris was going to ask him to be a district superintendent. But Gayle had her doubts. Tom was in trouble too often with the people that made those decisions. Gayle replied, "Oh, no. He knows better than that. He's not going to do that."

A short time later, Tom and Gayle return from a mission trip to Mexico with a group from their church. There is a message on the phone; the Bishop has tried to call him. Gayle asked what Tom thought that he wanted, and Tom replied, *"I don't know, but he's either calling me to ask me to be a DS or he's calling me because I'm in trouble."* Gayle asked Tom what he had done, automatically assuming that he was in trouble with someone; it seemed to be a pattern.

Tom was half-right. He wasn't in trouble; Morris did want him to be the Cookeville DS, which was in Livingston's district. When Tom told him that he wasn't sure about taking that position, Bishop Morris said that he had heard from God and God wanted him to do it. "Tom Halliburton is the only name that's come up. I am fully aware that this is probably the most controversial appointment that I will ever make. I want to offer you the opportunity to lead this conference. I know you can do it."

Tom begged him to reconsider. He didn't want to do it, and finally Morris agreed to give him twenty-four hours to pray about it. "I want you to hear it from God," Bishop Morris said.

Tom and Gayle prayed, but they were still unsure of an answer. However, Tom spoke with one of the church members, Don Ragland, on an unrelated matter, and Don informed Tom that he knew that he was leaving. He didn't know if he was leaving because he was going to die or what the reason was, and when Don found out about the appointment to DS, he told Tom it was better to be DS than to die.

Tom and Gayle prayed some more. They prayed together, they cried together. They didn't want to do this. Tom knew it could be difficult.

Tom called the Bishop back. *"Bill, I don't want to do this,"* he told him. Morris asked him if he had heard from God. Tom replied that he didn't think so. And Bishop Bill Morris said, "Well, I have, and you're going to be DS."

"Okay. I'll do it on one condition. I need to be the one to tell my church, and I want to do it now. I know that we don't usually let it out this early, but I don't care. I need to tell them."

No one expected Tom to become DS; most of the other pastors across the districts in Tennessee were surprised when he was appointed. He was the one who was always getting up with something to say at the Annual Conference, the one going against the grain. However, many shared his sentiments, wanting the church to continually strive toward the purpose given to the apostles: to bring Jesus to the people. One such friend and supporter said, "Let me tell you something about Tom Halliburton. There's not a lie in him. He's not going to lie to you. He's going to treat you the same, no matter what you look like, even if you're a super-liberal or you're not in agreement with him. He's going to treat you the same way that he treats everybody."

Tom and Gayle didn't have to move; they remained in the house they had built. The old parsonage housed an associate, and the next pastor had already purchased his own home. This was one of those times when a housing allowance was beneficial for both the pastor and the local church. The church doesn't have to worry about maintenance on a building, and the pastor can purchase a home.

As DS, Tom oversaw over 80 churches in the Cookeville district, including those in Crossville, Jamestown, Livingston, McMinnville, Carthage, and Gordonsville. Tom visited each one of those churches at least once during his time as their DS. Most of them knew Tom already, having been involved in the Emmaus movement in Livingston.

"It was a shock to my system to become DS. It's a privilege, sure, and I guess prestigious, but I never wanted it. I had never considered what a DS did to be that important to the local church. I had no idea what to expect. Thankfully, I had friends who were district superintendents in other districts, and with Bill Morris as Bishop, I had a lot of help and direction."

Tom spent his time getting to know his churches, finding out what they needed to be successful and share the news of Jesus Christ with their members and with everyone else. He placed pastors where they were needed, praying about every action. There were other, less pleasant responsibilities. Charges may be brought against a preacher, and the district superintendent must be involved in the proceedings. There are things done in confidence, and sometimes moral issues are at stake.

Tom was a successful DS; the churches under his care were appreciative of his dedication to their success and to his response to God's call.

As the time neared for a new DS to be appointed, Tom knew that Bishop Morris wanted to place him at Murfreesboro First UMC, but Morris was retiring, and another Bishop would be making the decisions. He wanted a church; he had continued to preach during his service as DS. Tom was an oft-requested speaker. Charismatic, he was popular with congregations and other district superintendents.

Tom set up an appointment to talk with the new Bishop as the time drew near for appointments. He told the Bishop that he was willing to go to Murfreesboro; he and Gayle had discussed it, and he thought it would be a good choice.

Tom was unexpectedly told that he would not be going to Murfreesboro; the Bishop said that the church would not be an option. The Bishop was yelling, and it both confused and angered Tom. Tom left the office, saying that he would return the next morning. He wasn't sure what he was going to do. He had been told that he and Gayle should pray about going to Murfreesboro, and they did. Tom wasn't pushing to go there; he only wanted to let the Bishop know that he would go.

Many options were at play. Tom and Gayle had been discussing the possibility of leaving the Methodist Church and forming their own church. Several warehouses in the area would be suitable meeting places, and they believed that several people would want to attend. Gayle was supportive and told Tom she would do whatever he decided.

Tom had a group of friends with whom he talked and prayed regularly. Asking them to meet him, Tom pulls into the parking lot of a local restaurant at 5:30 AM, and his friends come up to him, telling him that they have been thinking about him and praying for him. "We think that you don't need to do what you're thinking about doing. We don't know why you're mad. Pray on the way down there before you talk to the Bishop. Pray about it and then make your decision."

During the drive and while praying, Tom feels the Holy Spirit telling him to calm down. Gathering his thoughts, Tom feels his temper calm and makes his decision.

"I walked in there and calmly said, 'Don't ever yell at me like that again. If you ask me to do something, I'll be the first in line in a Minnesota minute. I will do what you ask

me to do because I respect you and I respect your authority. Why would you jump on me or chew me out after you've asked me to pray about something? You didn't even give me a chance to answer you. Are we good?"

The Bishop laughed and nodded. "That's why I like you, Tom," he said. He asked Tom to remain as the Cookeville district superintendent for another year, and Tom agreed.

Numerous changes occurred in Nashville during Tom's years in Livingston and as the DS for Cookeville. Meetings were held between the multiple district superintendents across Tennessee and the Bishop, specifically to discuss appointments and address a particular church that required significant assistance. McKendree United Methodist Church had been one of the premier churches in Nashville at one time, a very prestigious appointment. There were some problems, and although several different pastors had attempted to implement the necessary changes, none had been successful.

Everyone at the meetings was looking at McKendree and what they could do to create an atmosphere of change. No one wanted to go there, even though it would likely result in a financial promotion.

Tom listened carefully to all the discussions about McKendree. He understood that they were looking for someone to give the church at McKendree four years to develop a strong program there. A close friend, another DS, told Tom confidentially, "Several of us have thought that you need to go there. We think you can do this, can turn it around."

Tom did what he always did when he needs answers. He prayed. He listened to the Holy Spirit speak to him and followed God, as he promised he would. At the next meeting, when the issue of McKendree was brought up, Tom raised his hand. *"I sort of feel led to do this."*

There was no discussion. The motion was immediately made, "All those in favor of Tom, raise your hand." Tom tried to intervene and stop the vote, and perhaps discuss it further, but no one listened, and they proceeded to vote. Everyone raised their hand.

The Bishop turned to Tom and said, "I've been praying about this place. It's a great facility with a health center, a running track in the gym, and a magnificent sanctuary. There are no young people at McKendree, and I know of no one more equipped and led by the spirit than you, Tom. It's going to be hard; you're going to have people who are going to think the world's coming to an end when you walk in the door. I promise you, Tom, if you do this, I will be one hundred percent behind you. We will have your back."

Thankfully, and blessed, they did.

CHAPTER FOURTEEN
McKendree

The Halliburtons had been able to remain in the home they had built on the hill for more years than many pastors and their families can stay in one place. It was their dream home, and they prayed again for guidance. What to do? It was a difficult choice to move, and the Bishop had been clear in telling Tom and Gayle that they could remain in their home and commute to downtown Nashville. They both realized that it wouldn't work. Commuting to a church from such a distance would preclude the type of relationship that Tom needed to have with his congregants. So, they moved back to the town where Tom's life began, just a little further out in the suburbs of Nashville, off a road known as Tulip Grove.

Immediately after the appointment, Tom had a meeting with the Staff-Parish Committee. The district superintendent was going to introduce Tom to the group, allowing them to meet their new pastor. When Tom walked into the room to meet his new committee, the first thing he noticed was the large poster hanging on the wall. It was clear that a close friend had something to do with the poster, and Tom later discovered that the Bishop had been responsible. A blown-up picture of Tom when he was working undercover, beard and long hair in clear view. Adding to the photograph's interest was Tom's pose in the photo, arms crossed, holding a gun in each hand. Not precisely the presentation he hoped for, but also one that he claimed, knowing that God was always there, looking out for him.

The committee had to be concerned. Were they really going to have a thug as a pastor? What kind of people would he attract to their church? The oldsters certainly understood the duty of their church to minister to everyone, but they weren't sure they really wanted to attend church with some of them. The committee was likely not fearful, only truly concerned. However, it didn't take long for them to meet the real Tom Halliburton.

The first man who spoke didn't have a lot to say other than, "We were hoping for a younger person." At a time when Tom was around fifty years of age, it was clear that the church didn't realize they needed someone with experience, someone who could help them 'right the ship.' The purpose of the meeting was for the committee to meet Tom; the Bishop had already made the decision that Tom would be the next pastor for McKendree. The committee asked Tom to leave the room so that they could 'discuss his appointment there.' Although churches, to some degree, have the opportunity to discuss with their DS who they would like to have as their pastor, the decision ultimately rests with the DS and the Bishop. Appointments are primarily made with the intention of placing the best person in the position needed, and also combining that decision with what the church representatives request. When the committee asked Tom to return to the room, the head of the committee informed him that they had decided to appoint him as their pastor, which was a blessing since it would have been difficult to disclose that the decision had already been made.

"I started. I prayed. I walked those streets around McKendree. I prayed over Church Street; I prayed over every street around there. I prayed some more."

Tom met with Jordan Calloway, the business manager of the church. A dedicated Christian and very smart in business, he became a close friend of Tom and Gayle. Jordan asked Tom what they were going to do about the church; he knew it was in deep trouble. When Tom replied that he didn't have a clue, Jordan only said that he understood, because he didn't either.

Tom and Jordan began meeting each morning at a local restaurant to drink coffee and talk. Eventually, the associate pastor, Ron Patterson joined them. Having been there for two years, he knew everything that was happening in the church, and he knew what was not working. The three began brainstorming ideas.

"We came up with a lot of different ideas; some of them didn't work. Most of them didn't work. But one of the things I recognized was that we didn't have any children. We needed a contemporary worship service; I'm a contemporary worship guy. Most of the people there didn't think it was a good idea, but we did it anyway."

Kevin Sparkman was McKendree's 'computer guy.' A professional drummer, he had graduated from Florida State, but knew many of the music students at Belmont University. Kevin was able to convince many of those students to come and play music in the gym, providing an alternative to the traditional service held in the 'Bic Mac,' the name given to the beautiful, historical sanctuary that stands on Church Street in downtown Nashville. Young people began attending, and an event grew quickly, eventually becoming the largest Christian Hip Hop conference ever held. Tom was the instigator, admitting that he knew nothing about hip hop, but he saw possibilities where others were doubting. It was huge, and it was growing.

There were more meetings and more offerings. McKendree had been offering daycare options to parents before Tom became pastor there, and they were well-received. Unfortunately, the daycare director didn't attend church services, and neither did the children or parents. Many children were dropped off by their parents, often in expensive vehicles, and were only seen during daycare activities. There were additional meetings, including one with the daycare director. The director began attending the church services and became a true support person for the children, encouraging both them and their parents to participate in church activities. Tom began working with the children, giving them scripture to memorize and think about, as well as Christian educational activities that they enjoyed.

Unfortunately, many others at the church didn't like the new services being held and the music, even though it was attracting more and more youth to the church. Although attendance was also growing in the traditional service, there was a considerable amount of pushback from the members of the congregation, and all of it didn't involve the new services. One lady in particular is remembered well.

No stranger to different pastors and accustomed to the traditions that had been held at McKendree for many years, she told Tom that she was concerned about his delivery during his sermon. "That pulpit is one of the most sacred pulpits in the Tennessee conference; there are some people who call it the sacred desk." Tom told her that he had heard that before. She continued to reprimand him for not standing behind the pulpit. When Tom told her that it wasn't like him to stand in one place during his talk, she continued, "We just know you're going to try and bring in that group from the gym, and none of us are for that. We love our pipe organ and we love our tradition."

Tom continued his prayer; he continued his meetings, and he continued to try new things. *"There have been a lot of times that it was hard, but I was doing what I felt God wanted me to do. So, I kept on doing it."* The DS had asked Tom to be there to save McKendree, and he was determined to do so, even when working against the very people he was trying to help. Screens were put up in the sanctuary; Tom and the youth began knocking on doors, telling those that answered that the church was there for them; they were just around the corner. There were some new public housing units on Charlotte Pike. Tom and the youth knocked on every single door and spoke with everyone there. There were picnics, basketball games played, and Tom prayed over each event and each person there, sometimes publicly, sometimes privately. Tom prayed. And God opened the doors.

"I'm not sure what they wanted. We had almost doubled in attendance in the two years I had been there. Most of the people there were very happy with what was happening at McKendree. It was the people who had been there for years that weren't ready for anything different or new."

It was time to shake things up a little more. Using the screens for the first time, the youth were brought over to have their service earlier on Sunday, before the traditional service. What began with only twenty to thirty people soon blossomed into the largest service of the church.

There is still dissent. One professional person on staff is anything but pleasant. "Tom, I was here before you got here, and I'll be here when you leave. Most of us in the church honestly don't feel like you belong here. We want you to be happy, but we think you'll be happier somewhere else."

The person was wrong. 'Most' ended up being the few people he had convinced that what was happening at the church was going to change everything they liked about it.

The Bishop and DS had told Tom that they would have his back, and they did. Meeting with the Staff-Parish Committee, Tom explained that he was receiving negative support from one of the staff members, and everyone underneath that member. To continue the growth and fulfill what Tom felt God wanted for McKendree, change would be necessary. With the Bishop in attendance, Tom made his plea to the committee to vote.

A committee member was happy to inform Tom that the vote was certainly in his favor. Assuring Tom, and the Bishop, that the majority of the congregation loved what was happening at McKendree, they were happy to find a replacement for the staff member that would be told his services would no longer be required. There were a few disgruntled individuals, and some left the church, never to return; however, their absence didn't hinder the growth.

There were more people involved; the church's finances are growing. Many people from the Methodist Publishing House attended McKendree; Tom Halliburton was known there before he became their pastor. His mother, Ruth Halliburton, was a well-known figure at the publishing house, loved by everyone.

Tom and Gayle had moved to Old Hickory. Gayle had developed some serious health problems. Finally, with a diagnosis of MS, help arrived from Livingston. A friend and nurse, Connie Cates, aided both Gayle and Tom in ways to adapt to the changes.

Talking to families in the area, it wasn't very long before finding buses that would bring children to church was needed. Parents were happy for their children to ride a bus to church, and they hoped that once the children came home and told their parents about Jesus, the parents would also take notice and perhaps visit on their own, bringing their children with them.

The first Sunday that the buses were expected was a suspenseful one for Tom. He had prepared for this for several months. Teachers were lined up; classrooms were ready; the youth were working to help out. It was almost time to begin, and there were no children. Tom was anxious, and he did what Tom always does when he has concerns. He prayed. He prayed for all those who had prepared for the children; he also prayed for the children.

His prayer was interrupted by the big wooden doors at the rear of the sanctuary opening, and thirty-five children running down the middle aisle of the church. Most had never been in a church before, and it was hectic to finally have all of them seated in the front rows.

With joy and love, Tom talked to them about Jesus, and they were dismissed to go to their classrooms. Jack Norman, a prominent man in Nashville, and his wife were sitting in one corner of the sanctuary. Not one to talk a lot, Tom felt they had a good relationship. "Tommy boy, this is one of the greatest experiences I've ever witnessed," and Norman clapped Tom on the shoulder.

More miracles were in store. The church is crowded at every service. The Bishop is notably pleased with his appointment and tells Tom that he feels responsible for making such a good decision.

There were healings, and many people were saved and baptized. A drummer from a well-known band lived in Nashville. He had cancer and attended

McKendree. Once Tom and Gayle found out about his disease, Gayle went back to him during one church service and asked him to join her at the altar to pray. He did. He was healed.

One Sunday, a little girl approached Tom. He could see something moving around under her jacket. *"What have you got there?"* Tom asked. She pulled out this little puppy and told Tom that it was her dog. "Will anybody care if I bring it to church?" she asked. Tom told her about this one little old lady. *"Just don't let her see you with the puppy."*

Even in the midst of such growth, sorrow raised its head once again. Gayle's brother, Lanny, called one night from Florida. Lanny was an alcoholic and had dealt with that demon for quite a long time. He had been married and divorced twice; he had two children, a boy and a girl. Alcoholism had destroyed so much of his life, and he was hanging on by a thread.

Lanny had been living with another woman for several years, but she had given him an ultimatum: quit drinking or leave. He chose to go and was living in a camper.

The phone call began innocently enough. After speaking with Gayle for a few minutes, he asked to talk to Tom. Tom expected the usual, "Let's go fishing the next time you're down here," but that was not what he heard. Lanny said, "I don't know what to do anymore."

"I could tell he was in bad shape. I said, 'Lanny, wait a minute. I'm coming. We're going to come down there right now to see you, and we'll talk about it.' But he said, 'No, don't do it. Promise me you won't.' I asked him why he would want me to promise him something like that. He just said to wait a couple of days and to let him get some things together. And then we could come."

There was nothing Tom and Gayle could have done to change the events of the next few hours. Almost immediately upon hanging up the phone, Lanny went outside next to the camper, laid out a sheet, and shot himself in the head.

Her brother's suicide was a tragic loss for Gayle. Her faith and Tom's love were the supports that kept her MS partially at bay while she dealt with her grief.

Both Tom and Gayle were tired after three and a half years at McKendree. Gayle's diagnosis, her brother's suicide, and Tom's diagnosis of diabetes, along with some other physical problems, added to the stress and anxiety. Such feelings are not strangers to those with faith; certainly, pain and suffering are not.

McKendree UMC was growing quickly; young people were becoming involved. Tom and Gayle were both exhausted. Tom approached the Bishop and told him of his concern, and the Bishop asked Tom to begin his search for who should replace him at McKendree.

A powerful preacher, Steve Handy, was leading the Saturday night service. Tom told him to take that Saturday night service, get it together, and make it work. *"This church could be yours,"* he told Steve.

Pastor Handy was doubtful. A black man, he wasn't sure that the congregation would accept him. Tom told him they would; that many people in the church already knew him and liked what they heard. The Bishop agreed, and the announcement was made. There were very few people who left, as is often the case when a pastor change is made. Pastor Handy is still there, and the church is vital and continuing to grow. Tom is proud and honored to feel that he had something to do with the appointment.

It was time for something new for Tom and Gayle.

"One service at McKendree, a bus full of my old friends from the other churches in Livingston, and some others, came to hear me preach. They all come in together, there at this big, old, beautiful sanctuary filing in and sitting on the front pews. There were four or five pews full. I got up, ready to preach, and they pulled out their sunglasses and put them on. I lost it."

-Tom

CHAPTER FIFTEEN

DS (again!) & Hermitage UMC

That something new for Tom and Gayle wasn't so new after all. A different location, but a familiar position.

While Tom was busy convincing Steve Handy that he would, indeed, enjoy a welcome into McKendree UMC as their new pastor, the Bishop already had Tom's next appointment planned out. The one thing that Tom never really wanted to do – and he was being asked to do it again. This time, he would be the DS for the Nashville district. Tom trusted God; he knew there must be a plan. He would follow, and God would reveal His plan.

There had been several changes in the Nashville district during Tom's term at McKendree, and they had been living in Livingston previous to that appointment. Tom and Gayle had moved into a condominium in the Hermitage area, a short distance from busy Nashville, and the growing community of Mt. Juliet was just up the road.

Tom had served on the new Church Development Committee and had met with several preachers at St. Paul's United Methodist Church and Grace United Methodist Church, both in Mt. Juliet. St. Paul's had experienced tremendous growth and had outgrown their sanctuary and the parking availability, while Grace was a new church and struggling. The two were combined before Tom became the district's DS.

Jacob Armstrong, a young pastor who grew up in St. Paul's UMC, wanted to begin a new church in Mt. Juliet, near a rapidly growing area called Providence.

Tom and Gayle knew Jacob, and Tom had an inkling of why God had placed him in as DS. He had work to do and people to talk to. Jacob Armstrong started his 'congregation' in his own living room, and working behind the scenes, Jacob was able to arrange services in the Stoner Creek Elementary gymnasium.

The first time Gayle heard Jacob preach, she told Tom, "That boy's a young Tom Halliburton." Always supportive of Tom, Gayle admired his ability to testify and let the Holy Spirit speak through his words.

Tom prayed. Jacob prayed. The church grew rapidly. Tom warned Jacob about how hard it was going to be; he wanted him to be aware that there would be obstacles. The larger the church, the harder it becomes. And the Methodist conference wants to move you somewhere else. Having been the district superintendent for the second time, Tom knew how the process worked. Tom would have been happy to remain at any of the churches he had pastored until his retirement, with possibly the exception of McKendree UMC. McKendree UMC had been a different experience for both he and Gayle, requiring much that was both physically and emotionally draining in their church life and in their personal lives. When it was time to leave, they were ready to see what was next. But there was still work to do with Jacob and the new church.

A church building was constructed, and the church continued to grow. The Holy Spirit was working, and more and more people were coming to Providence UMC, where the mission was to 'help those who feel disconnected from God and the church find hope, healing, and wholeness in Jesus Christ.' A mission that was enjoying blessed success.

The Bishop and the cabinet, and the rest of the district superintendents, were behind Jacob and what was happening at Providence UMC. However, disquiet soon began to dominate the discussions. The Methodist Church was attempting to adapt to changing cultural times, adopting a different stance on biblical issues. Many balked at changes considered not in line with their biblical understanding.

It seemed as if the tide had turned, and many of the upper echelon of the Methodist Church would have destroyed what had been built in Providence UMC. Tom prayed, and prayed some more. He stood his ground, telling the Bishop and the cabinet that to force Providence to agree with them would be against the Holy Spirit's work there. Upset with Tom and his refusal to try to convince Jacob Armstrong to remain with the UMC, they notified Tom that it was time for him to retire or leave. The Bishop's answer was to place Tom at Hermitage UMC until his retirement date. Tom and Gayle began their ministry at Hermitage.

Tom Halliburton was a familiar name among many of the parishioners there; many of them had heard his testimony and were happy to have him lead them. Of course, with every new church, there are hurdles.

"I had preached two or three Sundays, and this lady sent me a letter. She said, 'If I wanted to watch a comedian, I'd watch Saturday Night Live. It's not what I expect in church.' I asked the church secretary about the lady, and she told me that the lady had been that way with everyone. So, then I knew what I needed to do. I called and asked her to come in. She did, and we had a great conversation. I told her that I didn't want to offend anyone; if I was talking about sin, it was my sin. I told her I was going to love her; I was going to love everybody. I asked her to give me a chance. After that conversation, we were fine. She wanted me to notice her; people who look to you to tell them about God, they want you to see them. That's how it should be. It's hard, sometimes, though."

Tom's problem with the district wasn't over, however. The pastoral committee had met and voted, unanimously wanting Tom to come back to Hermitage. But there was a problem; the DS hinted that everyone on the cabinet wanted Tom to retire. Tom balked at the message; only the Bishop could move him. In January, there was another meeting, and Tom was informed that the Bishop was very upset with him, allegedly over the issues within the Methodist Church across the United States. Tom was very clear about his feelings, and he felt that the church was bending to cultural pressures and not following biblical direction. Everyone, including the Bishop, knew that Tom and Jacob were close, and their expectation that Tom would have sway with Jacob was met with the opposite result. Tom agreed with Jacob. *"I knew that three or four years from now, something would come up and they would want to move Jacob to somewhere else, and that was simply not an option."*

The decision was made that Tom would remain at Hermitage until his retirement and then stay there to mentor another pastor. Tom could tell that there was little he could do to change any minds at the board level of the conference. He and Gayle talked about it, and Tom decided that the time to do something had arrived. Tom called the DS and told him that he would be retiring immediately. The Bishop called Tom and told him that he couldn't do it that way; he had to come and talk to him. But Tom stood his ground. *"I'm retiring in October."* The Bishop responded, "You can't do that." Tom retired in October, and in his subsequent conversation with Jacob, said, *"You cannot trust the system. Your relationship is with Jesus Christ, not with the Tennessee conference."*

The changes in the United Methodist church began in the 1960s and 1970s. Gaps between pastors were widening; cultural warfare was alive and prospering. Politics and religion were socializing, although both sides proclaimed them to be separate. The politics of the nation were influencing decisions in churches across the United States and the world.

"I always thought that someday I might leave the Methodist Church. It's a comfortable place to be in if you're a preacher. You're guaranteed an appointment for the most part; you're going to have a job. But it's not what I thought I would always do. I was not the fire and brimstone type, but my demeanor behind the pulpit, or in front of it, or beside it, was different than the traditional Methodist preacher. That's why my mother was never comfortable with my preaching. My brother was much more conventional than I. He wore a robe all the time. He used more liturgy than I did.

I don't feel that I left the Methodist Church. The Methodist Church left me."

There does not appear to be a place now in the Methodist Church for the conservative; there is little doubt that there has not been for quite some time. Pastors weren't members of their own church; they were members of the conference. The more liberal-minded pastors were connected and worked together, serving the conference. The conservative pastors were too busy to work for the conference; they considered their primary responsibility to be the families in their church. It seemed as if the conference became more important to the liberal pastors than the church they were pastoring. It became very political.

There are definitive differences between the liberal ministry and the conservative ministry.

"The liberal pastors do a cut-and-paste job of the Bible. They choose specific scripture to use, and other scriptures they reject. There are very few verses in the Bible that can stand on their own. You have to put the others in there, read before and after. One of the biggest issues in the Methodist Church was the fact that many lay people didn't know anything about scripture. There were few Bible studies.

I've always had a lover's quarrel with the Methodist Church. When I went into the ministry, I knew the Methodist Church. I had all these connections. My mother was at the publishing house. I met Gayle in the Methodist Church, and we were married in the Methodist Church. I realized that I was more fanatical than most of the Methodist ministers. Fanatical, charismatic, spirit-filled, call it what you want. I love Jesus, whatever that makes me."

CHAPTER SIXTEEN
Rags to Riches

If you asked Tom to count the things that are very important to him, he would count his relationship with Jesus as number one, with Gayle, his children and grandchildren following. You don't have to look too far to find the next thing on his list. It would be the big dog that is his constant companion wherever and whenever you see Tom. Rags was a youngster when he came into Tom's life. The perfect gift from a good friend, Mike Eller, Tom was surprised when Mike walked in with the beautiful lab on a leash. Mike, the owner of the golf course where Tom held a weekly Bible study, let go of the leash, and the dog, wagging his tail, went to Tom.

"*Whose dog is this?*" Tom asked.

"It's yours," Mike replied, and with that, became a forever dear friend in Tom's book of fantastic people.

Rags immediately recognized that Tom was his 'person.' He has been by his side constantly since the day Mike Eller brought him into Tom's life. When Tom goes out of town, Mike Eller, the faithful friend, watches over Rags.

Rags

Tom and I shared a true love of dogs and their unconditional love. Tom's favorite dog passed and I knew I needed to help Tom as he had done for me. I drove to Kentucky and rescued a yellow lab (Rags) from a kennel. I took Rags to the men's Bible study the next morning and released him...and he went straight to Tom. They haven't been apart since. Just as Tom rescued me and led me to Jesus; we rescued Rags and he found Tom.

   -Mike Eller, Hermitage Golf Course

Tom has always been a dog person. He remembers the dog he had when he was very young, called MP, because he was born on a military base. Tom loved MP and was fortunate to have her for many years. In her late teens, she had become blind and would sometimes get lost. Tom would go and get her and bring her back home. One day, she wasn't there any longer, and Tom couldn't find her. His mother tried to explain that it happened sometimes. If old dogs know they are going to die, they wander away somewhere to do that. Tom believed that story until he was seventy years old. His mother admitted that she had called the dog catcher the last time that MP had gotten lost and wandered into a neighbor's yard. When the neighbor called, his mother felt that it was time for MP to be put down.

"*What?*" Tom was shocked, even after all the years had passed.

"Well, honey," his mother said, "I didn't want you to know that then."

Tom replied, "*You could have told me. I'm seventy years old now, you could have told me before now. MP was my best friend growing up. I've had a lot more dogs as friends than I have people. Dogs love me. I love them.*"

Before Rags, Gayle and Tom had several dogs, each one growing old with them, and painfully, lost them to disease or old age. One particular dog, Prissy, is recounted with laughter. Prissy, a Dachshund mix, was in the habit of going outside in the early morning and disappearing for some time. Tom, deciding that he was going to find out where she was going, watched and followed. Prissy deliberately made her way to the neighbor's house behind them, where the door was held open for her, and she made her way inside. As Tom approached, he could see inside, and Prissy was sitting at the kitchen table, in a chair, with a piece of toast and jam sitting in front of her on the table. As Tom knocked and began to fuss at Prissy, the lady of the house patted the dog's tiny head. "Don't you worry now, Prissy. I won't let him bother you." Sometime later, Tom visited the same lady in the hospital. Approaching her bedside, she asked, "Where's Prissy?" Tom replied, "*Now you know I can't bring a dog to the hospital.*" The neighbor shrugged and told Tom that he could leave; there was no reason for him to be there.

Now there are two Halliburton dogs. Rags is dutifully trying to train Knox, Gayle's dog. Knox is a large, black and white mix of poodle and Burmese Mountain dog, and is just as attached to Gayle as Rags is to Tom.

Rags accompanies Tom almost everywhere he goes. Tom conducts a Bible study in a meeting room at Hermitage Golf Course in Old Hickory, Tennessee, early each Friday morning. Hermitage Golf Course is Tom's 'Cheers' setting – everyone knows his name, and they definitely know Rags. As the study begins, Rags makes himself comfortable at Tom's feet, and recognizing the benediction when Tom begins the ritual, Rags rises to make his way around the group to receive his final pat on the head before leaving for home.

Tom associates the last time he almost let his anger make him want to punch someone with his dog.

"I had Rags and Bubba, both big old labs. It was several years ago. I would take them out there on the ninth hole and throw the ball for them to go out and get it. So, this guy is out there yelling at the dogs. He gets in his cart and comes up the path toward me, yelling. He's saying that you're not supposed to have dogs on a golf course. Well, that was the wrong thing to say to me. He said that if I didn't get them off the course, then he would.

I told him that if he touched my dog, he would be sorry. He spouted off some more, and I told him, 'There is no point in you taking it out on me or the dogs because you hit a bad shot.' He kept yelling and took off on the cart heading up to the office. I was plenty mad, too. The more I thought about it, the madder I got. So, I got Rags and Bubba, and I walked back up to the office. The guy is in the pro shop yelling. He's talking about the man out there on the course with two dogs. These guys in the pro shop know me. They know Rags and Bubba. So, they lied to the guy and told him that the man with the dogs owned the place, and he could bring the dogs whenever he wanted.

I kept walking and went out to my truck. Here comes the same guy, and he wants to start yelling again. I had finally had enough. I told him to get back in his car and shut up, or he would have a hard time explaining to all his buddies at his favorite bar why he's all black and blue and that a seventy-one-year-old man beat him up. Well, he was drunk, but he got back in his car and left. I never saw him again."

Author's Note:
During many of our conversations, I was blessed to overhear Tom talking to Rags – who was constantly by his side during all of our conversations. Occasionally, Rags would place his big head on Tom's arm, and Tom would talk to him, as he does in the next quote.

"Ah, you want to eat now, don't you? You're eating too much, that's what the doctor said. Yes, you're a good dog *and I love you. You're going to heaven one day, aren't you, buddy? You might go there before me. Jesus made it right for us. I'm the one who brought sin into the world, not you. We humans. But you're going to heaven. I'm not sure about Knox, but we'll work on him, won't we, Rags?"*

Tom's laughter was mixed with Rags' own way of agreement, the panting of a happy dog.

Knox

had called his dad to let him know that Tom wasn't feeling well; something was wrong. Chad stayed with Tom for a short time, and realizing that Tom was unsteady and staggering, he called 911. Chad was concerned that Tom was having a stroke, and it was soon verified. Tom's left side was affected, becoming weak, and a series of mini-strokes was also discovered when Tom arrived at the hospital.

"I prayed when I had the stroke, sure, I prayed. But I wasn't scared. Things like that, I don't get scared. All the things that could happen, I'm just not afraid. Even when I was on the way to the hospital, and they're flying down the highway, I'm asking how fast they're going and cutting up with the medics. I wasn't afraid at any time. I prayed for healing. We know that when it's all said and done, God is the great physician, the great healer. It's God's will. I'm going to heaven, so I'm not scared."

Tom didn't skip a beat – he was back at his Bible study the following week. One Monday night remains in Tom's thoughts often. A young man came to the study for the first time. His name was Elijah. Tom especially liked the name and the Bible that the young man carried. An old, used Bible, probably the King James Version. The study was on the book of Romans, and God had touched Tom's heart with this young man, and Tom knew that he needed to talk with him after the benediction. Others were talking, asking Tom questions, and by the time he tried to speak to Elijah, he had left.

The next week, Elijah didn't show up.

"I told the rest of the group that I need to share that I'm sad about missing an opportunity to share with Elijah last week. I've been praying all week about him, but he didn't show up tonight. So, I'm going to pray all next week. Please bring Elijah back. I don't have to talk to him then, but I'm going to pray that he comes back so I can see him face to face."

He did come back the next week, and Tom was able to talk to him. Elijah had forgotten about the study the week before, and during their conversation, Tom helped Elijah find ways to search for a job. Tom offered this example as a time when he didn't do what God wanted him to do immediately, but prayer and perseverance ultimately prevailed.

"I want to be at best a wildcat with claws, not to hurt somebody, but spiritually. Spiritual claws to talk about my relationship with Jesus Christ. Now, some days I'm good. Some days, I'm really good. Some days, I'm really not good. Those days, it means that I'm not necessarily where I need to be with the Lord."

Besides Rags, Tom had another best friend, Jimmy Lewis. A fishing buddy, Tom and Jimmy became close when Tom was appointed to Cumberland City. One of the churches included in the appointment was St. Paul's Chapel. Jimmy attended there; he and Tom loved to fish, and they stayed connected over the years. Jimmy would come to town when Tom was leading his Bible study at the golf course on Friday mornings, attending the study and then often fishing in the ponds at the golf course. Eating lunch at the golf course restaurant, Jimmy was a regular and made the trip as frequently as he could.

Tom knew that Jimmy was having some issues with his legs, and when he hadn't talked to Jimmy in a while, and he had not attended the Bible study, Tom called. Unable to reach Jimmy, he spoke to his son-in-law, who informed Tom that Jimmy was in St. Thomas Hospital, in bad shape.

"When I walked in that hospital room, I knew right away he was dying. It was awful. He had some kind of terminal cancer."

Tom had been in many hospital rooms, many rooms where people were dying. This one was different. Tom was losing someone who had been through hell with him, helping him get through the days after

Jason's death. There were times when they were fishing, and the Lord offered them the friendship they both needed. When Tom first met him, Jimmy didn't attend church very often. Tom's testimony and leadership helped Jimmy come to know the Lord, and he became a leader of that little church. Now Tom's friend was dying, and Jimmy wanted to talk. Waiting until his hospital room was empty except for him and Tom, Jimmy began.

"I love hanging around with you, Tom, and one of the main reasons is that you are a godly man. I just want you to know that. But I'm ready to go. I'm not used to this. I can't walk in the woods, and I can't do anything right now. I'm not going to get any better. I want to pray with you."

He held Tom's hand and prayed, asking for forgiveness and proclaiming his love for the Lord.

Tom went back the next day, and Jimmy was worse. He remembered so many good times with his friend, and watching his decline was heart-wrenching. His favorite memories involved fishing, of course. There was an eleven-pound bass that Jimmy caught out of one of the ponds on the golf course. Tom and Jimmy thought that it was probably the biggest fish they had ever caught. They always threw them back, and a few weeks later, they caught the same fish. Weighing it in at eleven pounds, they laughed.

For anyone thinking of fishing at the Hermitage Golf Course – it is not recommended. You are not really supposed to do that. No one messed with Tom, of course. Most people probably thought Tom owned it. Mike Eller, the real owner, would likely laugh about it.

"The last time I visited Jimmy, he was really bad. He asked me to say a few words at his funeral, and of course, I told him I would. His death really hit me hard. His son-in-law later told me that Jimmy talked to the Lord constantly the night he died.

It's been a long time since I've been fishing. But there's something about fishing that either lends itself to quiet talk or just the silence that can only be experienced between really good friends. Jimmy and I would be fishing, and he would say something like, 'Remember the time you caught that fish that got plugged up in the net,' or something else. We always knew exactly how many fish we caught. Fishermen always know how many fish they catch.

One of the reasons I know that the story in the Bible about John and Peter fishing is true is because of this: Jesus was on the shoreline of the Sea of Galilee, and John and Peter had been fishing all night and hadn't caught anything. Jesus says, 'Throw your net on the other side.'

Well, that makes no sense at all, but they do it, and the net gets so full, they can't hardly bring it in. John describes all of this in the last chapter. (John 21:11) There's the interesting little part in there where he says, 'There was a miraculous catch of 153 fish.' Why is that important? Anybody who fishes could tell you, especially if it's a lot of fish, they know how many. You always know how many.

Fishing brings me closer to Jesus. Being outside does the same. When I walk, I'm closer to the Lord than any other time."

AFTERWORD

Early on, I came to a place as a believer where I knew I needed to fill in the blanks. I knew that I needed to repent. Repent of things that the devil tried to use to destroy me. I understood that my sins were burned away, but there was still ash left over. Growing up, filling up a stoker every morning and night, I knew that eventually I would have to clean out the furnace and throw away the clinkers. A clinker is where the skeleton of the fire is. You have to throw it away. When it came to my sin, I asked the Lord to forgive me, and I had to take the clinkers out of the furnace and throw the sin away. God prepared me for that, not because I'm worthy, but because He had a place in His Kingdom for me. I knew that I would need to take the time and effort to study the Word, apply it to my life, and live that kind of life. There was a simple word for me to get there. Grace. I don't understand it. I understand mercy. I understand, mostly, forgiveness. But I don't understand Grace.

I never really understood what it meant for my Lord and my Savior to save me and prepare me for a life led by the Holy Spirit. I don't want to do anything to dishonor that, although I do. I still have to repent. I stand before him blameless, blameless with great joy. I'm sure of that in my 'knower.' My knower is my Spirit; it knows it to be true. I'm not always sure of anything in my flesh. And I've had to put it aside. God's still working on me. When I'm not sure of how to serve him, which happens occasionally, I have to renew my relationship with Him. I do that, mainly, by studying First John in the Bible. It's a simple, short book. It has led me to where I am today. When Jason died, I could only do one thing. Read that book.

I've always prayed the same thing every parent does. 'Lord, don't let anything happen to any of my kids. Please don't.' Then Jason died. I have never been so disgruntled in my life. I didn't know which end was up. I couldn't pray. I said, 'Lord, I don't even know how to pray. I heard him answer. 'You don't need to.' He told me that there were a lot of people praying for me, for me and Gayle. I remember hearing that as clear as anything. Every event in my life that involved Jesus Christ has allowed me to grow in the Spirit.

I've had some dull times when things were happening. It's been harder for me in the last four or five months to understand what Jesus has for my life now. I'm sure that everybody who gets to be 79 years old probably wonders that. What's next?

I can't read as well as I used to. You could give me a 150-page book, and I could read it easily within a day and tell you chapter and verse all the way through. Now, I can't. If it's the Bible, I can, but another book that I haven't read before? I get frustrated. I don't think I'm nearly as sharp as I once was.

But! Once you are sure that Jesus Christ is Lord, you don't need anything else. The 'if' has turned into 'I know.' When did I know that I was going to heaven? The first night I accepted Jesus. I needed to know that somebody loved me and inspired me, and that was Jesus. I never questioned that. I don't question that today. That doesn't mean that I fully understand why and how things are. I can try to understand the infinite power and wonder of Jesus, but I can't even comprehend that very well. But I know what I know. It's inside; it's in my 'knower.'

I know his promises will maintain. He will maintain His promises in my life, and they'll be true. I'm not a covenant maker. I'm a covenant breaker. God is a covenant maker, and His covenant stands for an eternity. There's nothing I can do that changes that, because of Jesus Christ.

-Tom Halliburton

PS: MORE TREASURES FROM TOM

Author's Note:
A few extras that should be included in this book. Stories Tom told, some of his favorite things, and questions about being a pastor.

"I was on I-24 one afternoon, in the normal dead-stop traffic. I've been sitting there for a long time; there's a wreck ahead, and it caused a bad traffic jam. I pray when I'm stuck in traffic. I started praying, praying for lots of things. But suddenly, I'm not in my car any longer, I'm in heaven. It's a vision, a gift. I'm just a little kid, a kid when my daddy died. I walk into this big room, and it's a huge, sanctuary-like room. I look up and there's a throne. God is sitting on it. All of these things are flying around him. I thought they were little monsters, but I'm just a kid. Now I know; they were cherubim. Flying around his throne all the time, and saying over and over again, 'Holy, Holy, Holy.' God says to me, 'Come here, boy.' And I said, 'No, I'm scared.' It was frightening. It's a vision, but I'm just a little kid. That's how I feel. God looks at me, stands up, and comes down to me, and he says, 'Tommy, I'm gonna get

you.' And I said, 'No, no,' and God says, 'Yes, I Am.' I begin laughing, and we run around up there. Then he picks me up and goes and sits on His throne. He puts me in his lap. I can feel the holes in His hand, and I can feel where the spear went through his side. He tells me three times that He loves me, and then I'm back in the car. I'm me again, not a child. A vision, a gift from God."

****

"We are forgiven because of Jesus. I'm sure I've committed sins that I'd never even thought about, but I'm forgiven. If I didn't believe that, I couldn't stand in the pulpit, and I couldn't preach. The Bible is God's. It's perfect. Just because I don't understand it doesn't mean it's still not perfect. There are certain things that I just take on faith."

****

"At my Friday morning Bible study, the guys were talking about what they gave up for Lent. We were talking about the Ash Wednesday service, and they asked if I had given up anything. I told them that I had struggled with that. There are two things that I'm pretty uncomfortable with. They asked what those two things were, and I told them my anger and broccoli. So, I decided the best thing for me to do was to do away with broccoli."

Questions:

Q: Is it hard to find balance in your life when you're a pastor?

"I think a lot of pastors say they find it hard to make time for their families. That was always a priority for me. I expected them to be in church, and they were. They wanted to be. I've seen a lot of children of pastors who weren't involved in the church, but family should always be important. Before I was anything, before I was a pastor, there was one thing I always wanted to be. I wanted to be a father. There is absolutely nothing that I wouldn't do for my children, and they know it. As a father and pastor, it never became an issue for me."

Q: What is your favorite part of being a pastor, the very best thing?

"I would say the relationships that form among my congregants. Those Christian relationships are often the most challenging part of leaving a church and moving to a new one. Both times I served as District Superintendent, I was ready to return to a church. I missed that."

Q: Do you think God requires more of you as a pastor than he does of other people?

"Yes. My responsibility is to win more people to Jesus. With every contact I make, I have the responsibility to somehow witness Jesus to them. It became my responsibility to do that when I was saved that Sunday night. Maybe two to three weeks later, I felt it weigh on me."

Q: What's the hardest scripture to preach about?

"Here's what happens. You get up to preach, and your sermon is on tithing. And the person that the whole church has been trying to convince to come is finally there. He comes in, and you're going to preach on tithing. Well, you'd better change the sermon. You're not going to preach on that, not then. Because you don't want to run the guy off, it's the first time he's been in church for maybe fifty years, and he's sitting right there. If you preach on tithing, he's thinking, 'yeah, just like I thought, it's all about the money.' I was very blessed at all the churches I served. Financial issues were never a big deal. There were some churches that were poorer than others, sure. They were farmers and laborers, but they were Christians and givers."

Q: Where does God fit in with what is going on with the Methodist Church?

"I think it was John Wesley who said he was concerned about whether the Methodist Church would be around for very long. Me, I don't think God cares what's on the sign *out front. He cares about other things. It's not what the sign says, it's what is going on inside. You can see the churches that are blessed by God."*

Q: I've heard that most ministers prefer to do funerals rather than weddings. Why is that?

"Well, in weddings, there's a mother involved. There's a mother-in-law involved. There's a bride and sometimes a bunch of bridesmaids. And they all have a different opinion. I don't get any opinions at a funeral. I can do my own thing.

I do weddings, I really do like weddings. It's usually just the coordinator who starts telling me what to do, and I tell her that this is my area. I'll decide what I'm going to say. As long as I've talked to the couple and they say what they want to say together and I say what I want to, that's exactly the way it's going to be.

I've done weddings at lots of different places. A lot of them are on boats, mostly out on Dale Hollow Lake. All these boats get in a circle, and I'm in one and the couple is in front of me in another. I've done a wedding at Scarritt College; I did one in a chapel out in the woods; the bride and groom left the church to the song, "Happy Trails." As they left, these two guys pulled out their Colt 45s and started shooting. I've seen "Rocky Top" playing as the couple left the church. I've done weddings at the golf course; I've done baptisms at the golf course."

****

"My mother was probably surprised that I became a preacher, but she never really said it. I don't think she ever considered that I was really a preacher. My mother would take a bullet for me, and she was one of the most generous people you would ever know, but she was really uncomfortable in a lot of situations. When I was preaching, she would never look up; she would keep her head down. She told me once, 'You know you can't preach that way in just any Methodist church.' She just didn't get the charismatic part of it, you know, with the Holy Spirit moving and everything. She was fine with my brother, John, preaching; he was very traditional and conservative."

****

"This family asked me to do a funeral for their mother. I knew their mother well, and I asked them if I could tell them something that she had told me years before. They agreed, and I told this story. She had known me for years. She came up to me one Sunday after I had preached at Hermitage and said, 'You know, Tommy, of all of Ruth's boys, I never would have picked you to be the one that became a preacher, and now she's got two of you.'"

Favorites:

Q: Favorite Movie?

"I don't watch a lot of TV. I watch basketball and football. I like that **Antique Roadshow**. It's interesting. Not so much about the things themselves on there, it's how they got to be so expensive or important, I guess. I like the historical part of it. It's like art, this modern art. I don't get it. I did finger painting in the third grade; it looks like a lot of this modern art. And that piece of paper ends up costing $150,000.00. It's not for me, but still, I'm curious. I don't remember going to a lot of movies with my parents; we did go to the drive-in theater close to Inglewood. I saw a lot of westerns. **Yellowstone Kelly**, I remember that one. My very first date was with a girl named Carolyn Tubbs; we saw the movie **Guns of Navarone**. My mother drove us downtown to the Tennessee Theater. I didn't really get into movies until I was in the Air Force in London. I had two different part-time jobs while I was there. One was bagging groceries, and the other was mopping out the movie theater. I didn't have to pay to watch movies. The one I remember the most is **The Graduate**. I really liked that one, even though it wasn't really my style of movie."

Q: Favorite books?

"**As I Lay Dying** by William Faulkner, **The Old Man and The Sea** by Hemingway, and **The Art of Racing in the Rain** by Garth Stein. That's a good one because it's from a dog's perspective. **Nine O'Clock in the Morning** by Dennis J. Bennett. **Chasing a Lion on a Snowy Day** by Mark Patterson."

Q: Favorite songs?

"**Amazing Grace**" sung by Dan Vasc. I play it every night; it's on my phone. It's powerful. He's a heavy metal singer, but what he does with this song. Whew. He does "O, Holy Night," too. So good. I like everything by the group America. They were just starting when I was in England. These boys were all officers and enlisted men's kids. A lot of people thought they were from England, but they weren't. "Ventura Highway," "Horse with No Name," "Sister Goldenhair." These kids went to the high school there in England. I like Three Dog Night's "Joy to the World," and CCR's "I Ain't No Senator's Son." "Oxford Town" by Bob Dylan. Simon and Garfunkel.

Q: Favorite President?

"Harry Truman – 'The Buck Stops Here' – he took responsibility. In 1948, he supported Israel becoming a nation. It was a tough time for Israel, and he came *alongside them. I was always impressed with that. I've studied World War II, and Japan was a bureaucratic nightmare. There would have been even more killed if Truman hadn't done what he did. I liked Ronald Reagan, too. Everybody liked him."*

Q: Favorite Bible verse?

"Romans, Chapter 8:38-39. For I am convinced that neither death nor life, neither angels nor demons, neither the present nor the future, nor any powers, neither height nor depth, nor anything else in all creation, will be able to separate us from the love of God that is in Christ Jesus our Lord. And John 3:16."

Q: Favorite preacher?

"Billy Graham. I saw him in Nashville at Vanderbilt. He preached on salvation. The time that I saw him, it was about halfway through, and it seemed as if something tapped me on the shoulder. I heard the voice, but didn't see anyone. The voice said, 'This is good, isn't it?' It had to have been an angel. I've heard lots of other preachers who were really good. Bob Mumford, Jamie Buckingham. David Wilkerson – he wrote **The Cross and the Switchblade***, started the Times Square Church."*

Q: Some of your favorite times, how were they spent?

"Gayle and I had that house built in Livingston. We were up on a hill; real hills up there. We would sit on the front porch at night; it had a big front porch. We would listen to the sounds of the night, the noises in the trees, the flying squirrels. Watching the deer and the foxes that would run down the driveway. So peaceful."

Q: What advice would you give your younger self?

"I wouldn't change anything. I am where I am right now because of everything. I'm where I should be. Changing anything might change that."

Q: What are you most proud of in your life?

"My kids. All of them. The only thing I ever really thought about was being a father. I didn't have one to really remember, and that's what I wanted to be. I'm proud of my kids, all of them. Julie, Jason, David, and Mitchell."

Julie, Gayle, Mitchell, Tom
David, Jason

A little humor for a finale:

"Gayle and I were in Nashville leaving Vanderbilt Hospital. You know how you run into people you know in other places? It's so strange. This guy comes up to me and says, 'Tommy Halliburton! We thought you were dead!' He was one of my classmates at Isaac Litton; I haven't seen him in years. I laughed and said I wasn't dead yet. He asked me what I was doing now. You have to know, he knew me when I was pretty rough, fighting all the time, getting into trouble. I told him I was a preacher. He looked incredulous and laughed. I nodded, and said again that I was a preacher. He didn't believe me and looked over at Gayle. I had introduced them, so I guess he thought she would laugh or something. She nodded and assured him it was true. We talked for a few more minutes, not really catching up, just talking about stuff. As we were saying our goodbyes, he said, 'Tommy, if you don't care, I'm just gonna let everybody think you're dead or in jail or something. No one would ever believe me if I told them that you were a preacher.'"

ACKNOWLEDGEMENTS

This book has been a labor of love due to the patience and dedication of Tom Halliburton. Thank you, Tom, for bearing with me during the afternoons we talked, for easily answering my questions, for praying with me, and for praying for me. Following your journey has been a true blessing for me.

Gayle Halliburton is a constant source of strength, comfort, and encouragement for Tom, serving as a partner in life and in witnessing the power and love of Jesus. Thank you, Gayle, for allowing me to be part of your afternoons, and for the very dear friendship we all share.

Several people have read and offered help with editing. I owe a massive debt of gratitude to Priscilla Poag Wanamaker, who has offered encouragement and has been essential in providing the editing necessary to make this book the prize that it is. My husband, Lee Cundiff, has been my rock, offering encouragement and being so very patient with my 'do not disturb' moments of writing. Thank you, my love.

I also want to acknowledge my writing group. Meeting monthly when possible, we call ourselves the 'Rising Tides Writers,' and they have been so kind as to offer suggestions based on their experiences when I had questions about form and placement.

Finally, and notably, my deepest debt of gratitude goes to my son, Chad Lloyd. He reads all of my manuscripts and helps me focus on what's important. He handles all the physical editing and publishing with a beautiful, professional approach, and without him, this book would not be possible. Thank you, Chad, for allowing me to pursue my writing and place these pages, which tell the incredible spiritual journey of a man who loves Jesus, just as you do. You have made my writing possible. I love you dearly. My cup runneth over.

-Tricia Cundiff